"Kristallnacht" is the story of my family who lived inBreslau/Wroclaw, Germany/Poland during the tumultuous years of the 1920ies and 30ies.

Born the daughter of a well-to-do Jewish businessman, life was uneventful until the elections of January 1933. Hitler became "Reichskanzler" (chancellor) during that fateful month. Hitler's ascendancy to power ushered in a period of destruction of all human values and ended in the gassing of six million Jews throughout Germany and all of Europe.

My immediate family, which had been caught up in "Kristallnacht", during the night of the 9th of November 1938, was, through the grace of God, spared the last murderous deeds of Hitler's executioners, the S.A. and S.S. After many trials and tribulations we escaped in 1939 the hellish place that Germany had become. My parents' siblings were not so fortunate, but they shall be remembered forever.

RATEMP

Items should be returned on or before the last date shown below. Items not already requested by other borrowers may be renewed in person, in writing or by telephone. To renew, please quote the number on the barcode label. To renew online a PIN is required. This can be requested at your local library.
Renew online @ **www.dublincitypubliclibraries.ie**
Fines charged for overdue items will include postage incurred in recovery. Damage to or loss of items will be charged to the borrower.

Leabharlanna Poiblí Chathair Bhaile Átha Cliath
Dublin City Public Libraries

Dublin City
Baile Átha Cliath

Rathmines Branch Tel: 4973539
Brainse Ráth Maonas Fón: 4973539

Date Due	Date Due	Date Due
2 0 ... 2015		
1 0 MAY 2018		

Kristallnacht

Kristallnacht

A TALE OF SURVIVAL AND REBIRTH

CELIA ELKIN

KRISTALLNACHT, A TALE OF SURVIVAL AND REBIRTH

Library of Congress Number:		2004098150
ISBN:	Hardcover	1-4134-6918-3
	Softcover	1-4134-6917-5

To order additional copies of this book, contact:
Xlibris Corporation
1-888-795-4274
www.Xlibris.com
Orders@Xlibris.com
25931

This book is dedicated to my mother

"A WOMAN OF VALOR"

KRISTALLNACHT

NOVEMBER 1938

BRESLAU

GERMANY

Preface

Remembrance of events long past, but not forgotten.

Upon the urging of family and friends, I have decided to record happenings in my youth that shaped my life. This will be the legacy that I leave to my children and grandchildren who will now have an eyewitness account of what occurred in my family before and during the Nazi era in Germany.

DR. Celia Elkin, nee Cilli Zelmanowicz (c is pronounced ts in German)

Acknowledgements

To the many friends and relatives who encouraged chronicling my experiences when a young girl living in Hitler's Germany, I give thanks.

I would also like to thank my able editors, my sister in law Madelyn Zelman and my cousin Dorothy Gross. They as well as my sons read the first drafts of my manuscript with great love; they made valuable suggestions and constantly urged me to write more.

Thanks are also due to my friends Kenny, Sheila and Neil Gross who helped whenever something went wrong with my computer. My grandsons Andrew and Ross and my granddaughter Julie instructed me in the mysterious (to me) workings of my computer.

I give special thanks to my friends at Kinko's, Pat Robinson and John D. They aided with making copies of the many old photos I had and with duplicating the pages of my text. It enabled me to put together bound editions before publication of my book.

Most important were the many phone calls from my brother Martin. His great love and unending support, supplying me with reminiscences of events that occurred after my father and I had left Germany, were invaluable.

My sister has to be thanked also, for she contributed a few interesting details to my memoirs.

Part I

Growing up Jewish in Germany before
Kristallnacht, November 1938, Breslau,
Germany

Chapter 1

Earlier in 1938 my piano teacher, Fräulein Epstein, had given her usual recital with most of her students. As in the previous year, the performances were reviewed by the much feared music critic of the Jüdische Gemeindeblatt (Jewish Community newspaper), a weekly which was widely read by the Jewish population of Breslau (now Wroclav). Entitled "Schülerkonzert"(Student Concert), the review began thus: "Like last year's evening concert, the one given the previous week by the students of the Breslau piano teacher Lotte Epstein was crowned with great success. It was obvious that the youngest as well as the more advanced students had received solid instruction in technique as well as in questions of style and aesthetics. The listener had the feeling that serious work was done here. Many students who had played the year before were showcased again. The greatest progress could be heard in the playing of Steffi Ehrenberg, Heinz Kaufman, Klaus Lachmann, Richard Heyman and in particular Cilly Zelmanowicz, who gave the most mature and advanced performance playing the Mendelsohn G minor Concerto and the A flat major Ballade by Chopin."* It was the very last time that such a delightful concert evening could be planned, much less executed. Although my piano studies with Fräulein Epstein continued, literally, to the bitter end, life as I had known it in Breslau ceased to exist.

*translation from German
copy of Original
review

1938

Schülerkonzert.

Auch der diesjährige Vorspielabend von Schülern der Breslauer Klavier-pädagogin L o t t e E b s t e i n war von schönem Erfolge gekrönt. Der Wert des hier erteilten Musikunterrichts liegt zunächst in der soliden Technik, die jeder, selbst der kleinste Schüler auf den Weg mitbekommt; aber nicht minder auch — bei den Größeren — in der sicheren Bewältigung der Stofflichen, die einer sehr sorgsamen Unterweisung in allen Fragen des Stils und der Aesthetik zu verdanken ist. Der Zuhörer hatte das Gefühl, daß hier ernste Arbeit geleistet und nur das erstrebt worden war, was der einzelne, seinem Alter und seiner Ausbildungszeit entsprechend, überhaupt zu geben vermag. Unter diesen Voraussetzungen wurde das Lyrisch-Poetische ebenso erschöpft wie das Virtuose. Die wieder sehr lang geratene Vortragsfolge nannte hauptsächlich Schüler, die auch im vorigen Jahre aufgetreten waren. Am deutlichsten spürte man die Fortschritte im Können und in der Auffassung bei Steffi Ehrenberg, Heinz Kaufmann, Klaus Lachmann, Richard Heymann und namentlich bei Cilly Zelmanowicz, die mit einem Konzertsatz von Mendelssohn und der As-dur-Ballade von Chopin die reifste Leistung bot.   Hff.

Since Aryans were no longer permitted to work in our household, my mother and father came to rely heavily on me, the eldest of four at that time (1938). Another brother, Bubi, had been run over in 1926 by a trolley car. He and I, then two and three respectively, had gone for a walk with our maid. I was holding on to her right hand, he to her left, when suddenly he wrenched himself loose and dashed into the street right in front of an oncoming trolley car! A throng of people gathered immediately. He was pronounced dead on the spot. They all proceeded to my house to inform my mother of what had just happened. She started screaming hysterically, pulled on her overcoat and ran to the local morgue. This dreadful event which I witnessed, almost like a dispassionate bystander, has remained with me for the rest of my life. I can call up the scene from my unconscious to my conscious being at will.

Cilli, perhaps, age two with distant
relative of my mother's.

Cilli (5th from left, front row) and Bubi (front row center) at nursery school; "Tante Edith" standing with baby and aid.

   I do not recall who the other children were, nor did I know them in later years.

Breslau, circa 1925

Family Portrait
Cilli and Bubi with parents

Family Portrait taken in Breslau circa 1925;
Cilli and Bubi with parents

Bubi and Cilli with Dad

The days that followed were lonely ones. I missed my playmate, my brother Bubi. Our new maid Marta was a kind and loving soul. She would play games with me, tell me stories, and scratch my back, which helped me to fall asleep at night. I was heartbroken when she had to resign her position with us for personal reasons.

I learned to crochet an activity I enjoyed very much. On beautiful spring days I often sat on the balcony alone, crocheting anything from doilies to decorative pillow covers. The balcony connected my parents' bedroom to the kitchen, bypassing the "Wohnzimmer" which served as both a dining and family room. In winter, the huge stove standing in one corner of the "Wohnzimmer" was lit each afternoon by one of the maids. There was a stove in every room. The stove would provide warmth all night long, but by morning, the burning coals now grown cold and turned to ashes, were removed by one of the maids.

The most imposing stove was located in the formal dining room. It reached from floor to ceiling and was in keeping with the elaborate decor of the silk-papered walls and the wine colored, patterned Persian rug. Two gilded ornate doors secured by a gilded chain had to be opened to light a fire in this stove. It was used only on special occasions.

There was always something going on in the courtyard below the balcony. Every now and then a beggar would make his way through the side entrance into the courtyard and start to sing. People would throw coins down to reward him for the singing. Or I could watch Meta, our last maid, bring laundry down to the laundry building located in a corner of the courtyard. Once a week she would spend all day in the laundry building. She loved all that scrubbing and washing and bleaching and always reminded my mother to be sure to enter our name in a book, which was passed around among all the tenants, to reserve the laundry building for the day she wished to do laundry. When she had finished, she would carry the laundry up to the fifth floor. A door opened into a huge loft where the wash was hung to dry. This large loft had no windows, just openings permitting air to blow in to facilitate the drying process. When the laundry was dry, Meta would iron every single piece. Additionally, tablecloths and sheets were taken across the street and run through an electric mangle to give them a really smooth look.

The courtyard became the center of attraction and activity during the holiday of Sukkot, which is celebrated in October and lasts eight days. A week before Sukkot, my father engaged workmen who put up a Sukkah. It was a wooden structure with Sechach (branches) placed loosely over narrow strips of wood, the latter serving as a roof. This makeshift hut was meant to remind the children of Israel that God had led them through the desert for many years before bringing them to the Promised Land. We youngsters were busy collecting chestnuts, which we strung up on heavy threads to make long bead type decorations which we then hung on the inside of the roof. The best part of this holiday was eating all our meals in the Sukkah. Of course, if it started to rain hard, we would have to hurry and bring everything upstairs. We didn't mind that and everyone pitched in with the chores.

The apartment house across the street from us, the "Freiburgerstrasse 24" was twice as large as the building we lived in. It was jointly owned by my father and my uncle and had a Sukkah with a retractable roof. When the weather turned bad, the roof was simply closed. In fact, the Sukkah remained in the garden all year long with the roof closed and served as a summer house or a place where we could play hide and seek or cops and robbers. My siblings had not yet arrived on the scene, so my playmates were my cousins and some of the children living in the building.

My father and uncle Lipman, who could not return to Poland because they had fled the dreadfully anti-Semitic Polish military, longed to see their mother. They jumped at the chance to meet with her in Danzig (now Gdansk), a free city since Hanseatic times. Their good friend Victor Byrszonski was to be married in Danzig. The bride, traveling to Danzig from Skerniewice accompanied by her sister and two of my aunts, would bring along my grandmother. Although barely five years old, I was taken on this trip by my father and uncle. In order to get to Danzig from Germany, the train had to traverse the so-called "Polish Corridor," running north and south from the Baltic Sea. One of Hitler's demands in the 1930s dealt with the Polish Corridor, which he wanted in toto for Germany. The whole area now belongs to Poland. The train made one stop somewhere in the Polish Corridor. Being a poor traveler, I became ill and wanted something to drink. My father opened a window to see if he could get some water for me but was told by a railroad official to close the window. No one was permitted to leave the train or open a window during this stop. That was the condition under which this train was permitted to travel through

Poland to Danzig without passengers being required to show passports. I survived my feeling of nausea and felt better the minute we got off the train.

The wedding took place the day after our arrival. It was a traditional Jewish wedding. A canopy or covering draped over four posts was held up over the couple and the rabbi who performed the wedding ceremony. It was the first time I had ever witnessed a couple being married. I noticed that after the rabbi had pronounced them man and wife, the groom had to step on a glass. The symbolism escaped me at the time, but I have since learned that breaking the glass is meant to serve as a reminder of the destruction of both Temples in Jerusalem. In the midst of all the festivities and gaiety surrounding a wedding, Jews must never forget the sorrow the Israelites felt when their Temples were destroyed and they were dragged away, first by the Babylonians in 586 B.C.E., then by the Romans in 70 C.E.

We remained in Danzig a few more days during which we took my grandmother on an excursion to a resort on the Baltic Sea named Zobot. A band was playing, and I recall walking up to the band, standing behind the conductor and imitating him. Everyone was amused by the spectacle of this little girl conducting the band from behind the conductor. My grandmother smiled at my antics. She also smiled because she was so happy to see her two sons who lived in Germany. It was the last time Lipman and Isak saw their mother.

©

The two brothers Lipman and Isak;(Isak, the youngest of seven, sitting with book in hand and my father). My uncle perished at Auschwitz.

Chapter 2

In April of 1928 a new brother was born. I remember the day it happened, for no one had thought of taking the five-year-old out of the apartment. We lived on the Antonien Strasse at that time. There, with the aid of her midwife and after much travail, my mother finally gave birth to a son. They named him Martin. I loved him instantly and still do.

In the summer of the following year, my baby brother, the new maid, my mother and I were dispatched to a lovely resort called Obernick. Every afternoon we attended a performance in the park. The local "Kapelle" (small orchestra) under the baton of the highly esteemed "Kapellmeister" (conductor) would play popular tunes of the time. Occasionally we were treated to a soloist, a singer, such as Benjamino Gigli or Richard Tauber. These afternoons were truly enchanted. At times, my mother would tell Grete to take a walk with my baby brother and me. We did this gladly and headed straight for the surrounding mountains. My mother had no idea that we had invented a new game, which entailed letting the carriage roll down hill while we ran after it! The maid had about as much sense as I did then and it was so much fun. Thank God, nothing untoward happened. On the weekends, my father would come to stay with us and enjoy the fireworks that took place every Saturday night.

In the spring, before the arrival of Martin, I was enrolled in Fräulein Brandt's "Privatschule" (private school). Being five and a half years old, I was given the usual "Ostertüte" (horn of plenty), a large cone shaped bag, filled with all kinds of sweets to make the beginning of school appealing. The school year started at Easter time. Photos were taken of me holding my Ostertüte and being otherwise outfitted with a lunch bag and a "Rückenmappe" (backpack).

The four years at Fräulein Brandt's Privatschule were pleasant. I was brought there every morning and picked up, usually around 1:30, by my mother. I recall that I had not particularly cared to eat my lunch consisting of a "Schnitte" (sandwich). Thus it was often still in my lunch bag when I returned home. My mother had noticed this and was concerned. She went to see Fräulein Brandt without mentioning it to me. What a surprise when on the following day, Fräulein Brandt turned to me in the middle of class and said, "Cilli, have you eaten your lunch yet?" Of course, the answer was no, whereupon I was told to eat my lunch right there and then. I was greatly embarrassed, but did what I was told to do. Never again did I bring my lunch home.

In my second year at Fräulein Brandt's Privatschule I was rushed into a cab one morning along with my mother, her midwife and my father. We were headed for the hospital, but there was enough time to drop me off at school. Half an hour later my father appeared at my school to inform me that I had another brother to be named George and that George had almost arrived in the cab!

George was a beautiful but noisy little guy. He did a lot of screaming and what later passed for singing at nighttime. He made such a racket when it was time to go to sleep, he had to be put in a separate room and not in the "Kinderzimmer" (bedroom for the children) which I shared with Martin and the maid who looked after us. About a year and five months after George's hurried entrance into this world, my sister Regina was born. We now needed two maids, one, a "Kindermädchen" (children's maid), the other, a cleaning maid. Both of them were given one room located approximately ten steps above the rest of the apartment. (We now lived on the Freiburger Street in my father's apartment house.) The room was accessible from the vestibule, which was furnished with two easy chairs, a small round table and a "Garderobe" for hanging up outer garments. A mirror graced the Garderobe, allowing visitors to check their hairdos and makeup. Fräulein Breslauer, my brother George's violin teacher, always ran a comb through her short dark hair before entering the formal dining room where she would give George his weekly violin lesson.

Fräulein Breslauer standing in black dress
on extreme left with her violin students
after a recital. My brother George in front
row with his arms around two friends. He
is wearing a white shirt and white knee
socks.

Cilly with Ostertüte, Rückenmappe
and lunchbag

Cilly and Martin possibly at 9 and 3
½ years of age.

The maid's quarters had a window which allowed them to see who was at the front door. They had received strict instructions to tell whoever might arrive in the middle of the night and knock on the door that my father was not there. And, indeed, on many nights he slept elsewhere to escape the nightly beatings of Jews, which began in 1933 as soon as Hitler became "Reichskanzler"(chancellor). Berel Abramowicz, my father's friend and tenant, who lived with his family in the apartment on the "Hochparterre," (more or less what we would consider a mezzanine floor), did not escape the hoodlums who reigned supreme at night. We could always tell when they had pulled him out of his apartment and beaten him to a pulp. For days after, his face would be all black and blue.

Despite these ongoing acts of violence and terror, I started taking piano lessons. My music teacher was a thoroughly dull and pedantic man. He lived down the street in an apartment house next to the one in which my aunt and uncle lived. I learned to read notes and some of the rudimentary items: scales, chords and signatures for the various keys. Twice a week I walked to his apartment with my music under my arm, looking around to see if my cousin Isel was lying in wait for me. He was a year younger and loved to hit me when no one was looking. I am not sure why. I dreaded encountering him. Much later, he was sent out of Germany to England on the "Kindertransport," the name given the life saving initiative undertaken by the British on behalf of Jewish children. Apparently the British knew what was happening in Germany. The fortunate Jewish children who were taken out of Germany into England through the Kindertransport were saved from the gas chambers, but many never saw their loved ones again.

Isel (later called Jitzchak), since he had very blond hair and looked more German than Jewish, was not well treated in England. The suspicion that he might be German remained strong. After the war, according to my cousin Shemaryahu (Sam), Jitzchak and some 2000 other Jewish refugees were sent to a DP camp in Australia. From there he came on an Australian warship to Palestine. Shemaryahu wasn't sure if Jitzchak jumped ship or, as he later maintained, got there quite legally. He became a member of the Haganah and there was united with his older brother Shemaryahu, the only other survivor of that branch of the family. Their parents, my uncle Lipman and his wife "Tante Hella"(Aunt Hella), as well as their sisters perished in Auschwitz.

The two families: Uncle Lipman standing in center; to his right his brother Isak, to left of him cousin Harry (who had come from Poland to visit); In the front row from left to right: Sam (Shemaryahu), Isel (Jitzchak), Aunt Hella, cousin Regina, my sister Regina held by my father, my mother Gitel, myself with book in hand; sitting on little stools my brothers Martin and George.

Chapter 3

Sam, now Shemaryahu Talmon, a noted Bible scholar and Professor Emeritus at the Hebrew University in Jerusalem, was two and a half years my senior, and I considered him to be more of an older brother than a cousin. One day he suggested that I come with him to a gathering of members of the Mizrachi, a Zionist organization. The meeting was held at the "Jugendheim," a place where different Jewish youth groups would get together on Saturday afternoons. I liked the people I was introduced to and joined a group led by Hanne Pinczover. We had many discussions on topics ranging from Zionism to free will and predetermination. When the sun set, all the groups would gather in a large room and sing Hebrew songs until it became really dark. Then someone would make "Havdalah" (prayer said at the end of the Sabbath) and the lights were turned on as the Sabbath was now over and a new week had begun. We greeted the beginning of the new week by singing "Shavuah Tov" (have a good week) and dancing a "Horah" (an Israeli dance).

Before long I was asked to be the leader of a group of girls only about a year younger than I was. My mother was strongly opposed to this, telling Hanne Pinczover that I was too young to be leading a group. She was also concerned about the possible political consequences of being a leader of a Mizrachi group. Hanne convinced her that there was no danger and that I was a born leader, not too young to undertake this assignment. Hanne won out and I did indeed become the leader of about a dozen girls. (I may have been twelve or possibly thirteen years old at the time.)

I didn't know all that much about Jewish history or Theodore Herzl but began to read up on these subjects so that I was able to give talks to my girls, particularly about Herzl. I explained how he had come to be known as the "Father of Zionism," the ideology that advocates the return of the Jews to Palestine. Herzl, a Viennese Jew and a journalist, firmly believed that the persecution of Jews would cease only if they again had a land they could call their own. And what would be more natural than to have them return to Palestine, the land God had promised them in the Bible, the land they had inhabited until they were defeated by the Romans in the year 70 CE, dragged away to Rome, and sold as slaves. Herzl had considered other alternatives on the subject of how to end the persecution of Jews. At one point he wanted to march all of them down to the Stephanskirche (famous church in Vienna) and have them baptized. Another solution he thought of was having them establish a country for themselves in Uganda! None of these ideas appealed to his compatriots. The only idea, which took hold among the Jews, was that of returning to Palestine. They always ended their Passover prayers with "next year in Jerusalem!" I asked the girls to write reports about the Jewish history that they had just learned and to submit the written reports to me at our next meeting.

These weekly afternoon meetings at the Jugendheim were, fortunately, undisturbed by the Nazis. Indeed Heydrich, the head of the SS at that time, actually welcomed the Zionists whose main thrust it was to convince Jews to leave Germany and immigrate to Palestine where they could reestablish a homeland. This idea was only welcomed until the Germans thought of a "better" way of disposing of the Jews. The so called "final solution" of gassing Jews in the extermination camps of Auschwitz, Buchenwald, Dachau, Treblinka, Maidanek and others was discussed at great length by the participants at the infamous Wannsee conference in January of 1942. Chaired by Heydrich and attended by Eichmann and other high-ranking Nazis, the conclusion reached by all present was that gassing the Jews would be preferable to shooting them although the latter method had just been successfully tried and completed in the massacre of about 27000 Jews in Riga, Latvia. (See: Lucy Dawidowich, "The war against the Jews 1933-1945").[1]

[1] Lucy Dawidowich, "The war against the Jews 1933-1945", Bantam edition, 1976, pp.182,183

This picture postcard shows the mansion
where the infamous Wannsee conference
of 1942 took place. It was mailed to me by
my brother Martin, when after sixty some
years, he visited Berlin with his wife Lois.
The mansion is now a museum that houses
the various instruments of torture used on
the Jews in the many concentration camps
which existed in Germany and throughout
Europe in the 1940ies.

To get back to earlier times when my cousin Isel was my nemesis and I told my parents how afraid I was of him, they decided to engage a piano teacher who would come to our house. (Isel, who had been considered a candidate for parachuting into one of the Balkan countries and trained for a certain period of time in a parachuting camp, turned out to be a very loving and family oriented man. This I was told by my son Rodney and other relatives who had visited him in Israel).

The teacher my parents chose was a lovely woman, tall and thin, named Fräulein Lichei. Her father had been a General and she, now a single female getting on in age, was supporting herself by giving piano lessons. The music she introduced me to was made up mostly of tuneful waltzes, which I played with great speed and abandon.

Even though the playing was somewhat sloppy, she would write "ausgezeichnet" (excellent) on each piece and give me a great big hug. And yes, she was not Jewish, strictly German. I still have the music books. In retrospect, it seems ironic that this negligible music made it out of Germany with us when so much else was left behind.

I would have been perfectly happy to continue with Fräulein Lichei. However, one day my father brought one of his business associates to the apartment, a certain Herr Neumann, who was accompanied by his wife. She knew a thing or two about music. As was his custom, my father asked me to play the piano for his guests. I did and Frau Neumann exclaimed: "My God, this girl has talent, but she must have a better teacher!" And thus

Frau Neumann, who did not have children of her own, took over the supervision of my musical education. She brought me to Frau Guttman-Platau, a well-known pianist and music teacher who happened to be the sister of my then current biology instructor. I was now attending the "Rehdiger Jüdische Real-Gymnasium", after an anxiety-filled year at the Cäcilien Schule, an Oberlyceum (a high school for girls). To get to the Cäcilien Schule, I had to walk about twenty-five minutes, passing along a moat, which encircled the whole inner city and was a leftover from medieval times. (Much fighting had taken place over hundreds of years in Silesia. The Austrians, the Russians, the Poles and the French all considered Silesia with its fortress Breslau a conquest worth fighting for.) The portion of the walk winding along the moat was enjoyable. But then I had to cross over to a main street where kiosks (Litvassäulen) advertised the latest movies as well as the weekly edition of the "Stürmer," a scurrilously anti-Semitic publication. It depicted what can only be characterized as ugly caricatures of Jews; all had big long noses and scruffy beards. All were accused of being crooks, sub human, and in every way the most contemptible of beings, not worthy of inhabiting this earth. Although repulsed and horrified by what I looked at and read, I couldn't help stopping at the Kiosk every time I went past there. I seemed to have a curious fascination with what was shown.

In class I always felt uneasy and out of place. Only five Jewish girls were among the forty or so students, and the teachers made sure to let everyone know who they were. They called on us with great disdain and obvious disapproval. On a few occasions all classes had to assemble in the huge courtyard outside the school building to listen to the "Führer" (Hitler) speak. His ranting and raving voice came blasting over a loudspeaker one dreadfully hot day. I recall becoming physically ill and passing out. When I came to I found myself on a stretcher inside the school building and was told to go home.

A particularly unpleasant week was the time before Christmas. Everyone who was not Jewish was busy making drawings and ornaments for the holiday. They were looking forward to celebrating it. The teachers did not include us in this activity and barely tolerated us in the classroom. They often pointed out to the other girls that Jewish girls did not belong in a room with racially pure Aryan girls. I could not have been more tense and filled with trepidation, wondering what was coming next. The teachers had been among the first to join the Nazi party for it meant more good teaching jobs opening up for them. The openings had been created by the dismissal of Jewish teachers and professors from their university positions as soon as Hitler came to power in 1933.

My parents realized that my schooling had to be continued elsewhere. They transferred me to the Rehdiger Jewish Real-Gymnasium, a coeducational school attended only by Jewish children. Here I began studying Hebrew as well as French. Within a year Latin was added to the curriculum and a few years later English. I loved

all the subjects and was thriving in the new
protective environment.

Some days I would walk to school with my
friends, on others we would go by bike, and
occasionally I would hop onto the streetcar. Our
principal, a tall, handsome, red haired man, who
looked more like a Viking than a Jew, as depicted
by Julius Streicher in the "Stürmer," would stand
on the steps leading up to the entrance of the
school building in order to catch the latecomers.
Their names were duly entered in his notebook
and they were given a talking to. Three such
warnings would trigger a note to our parents,
something none of us wanted.

Each lesson lasted forty-five minutes,
whereupon the bell would ring. We would all run
into the schoolyard where we could either snack
on some food we had brought to school or if we
had a completely free period, we would organize
a ballgame called "Völkerball." It required two
teams, each with a team captain. The team
captain would stand behind the opposing team
to catch the ball, (a fairly large one made of
leather) which had been thrown to him by one of
his teammates. He would then throw it back to a
player on his team, over the heads of the opposing
team. The ball would go back and forth until
someone on the opposing team was either hit (and
thus out of the game) or was able to catch the ball
and start throwing it over our heads. The team
that did not lose all its players won. I loved this
game almost as much as going ice skating on the
moat in the winter, when the waters froze over
and the public was permitted to skate and waltz

along on the ice to music played over a
gramophone. It gave one a sense that all was right
with the world.

Every semester we had German classes as well
as mathematics and either biology or physics. We
also studied European history, geography, music
and drawing. Frau Dr. Blum, my biology teacher,
was told by her sister that I had begun to study
the piano with her and mentioned that I seemed
rather talented. Frau Guttman-Platau instructed
me for approximately a year. Her husband had
decided to immigrate with his family to Palestine,
as the country was then called. He could no longer
tolerate all the speeches, all the "Sieg Heils," and
all the marching, when the brown shirts (S.A.,
storm troopers) would parade twelve abreast
through the streets carrying torches and yelling
"Juden Raus" ("Jews get out"). My uncle Meilech
and his wife Sora, visiting us on their way from
Poland to Chechoslovakia where they were going
on an extended vacation, found the marching and
yelling and singing of the "Horst Wessel Lied"
particularly abhorrent. Looking down on this
scene from one of the large windows of our formal
dining room, my uncle turned to my father and
asked: "How can you possibly remain in a country
where this is not only tolerated, but encouraged?"
Little did my uncle know then that in about three
years Poland would be overrun by the same
marching Nazis and that most of the Polish Jews
would perish either in the Warsaw Ghetto or in
Auschwitz. My father's two other brothers, his
sisters, nieces and nephews as well as my mother's
twin sister, her husband, my maternal

grandmother, my mother's youngest sister Charne
and her family, my mother's oldest brother, uncle
Chameier, his wife, daughter and one son all
perished at the hands of the Nazis.

My mother had wanted to leave immediately,
as soon as Hitler came to power in 1933, especially
since my father was one of the first stateless Jews
(literally, a person without a country) to receive
an "Ausweis," an official letter of expulsion. He
was informed that his presence in Germany was
no longer welcome and that he was to get out of
Germany within a week or so. He was also told
that he could take only 50% of what he owned
with him. Having achieved financial security and
a fine reputation as a businessman (in whose
establishment only the best woolens were sold and
made up to order by one of his many tailors,) my
father was not at all inclined to pull up roots and
move his family to another country. Turning to
my mother, he asked her, "Where would you want
us to go? We have all these young children and I
make a very good living here, despite all the
uncertainties and violence surrounding us." She
didn't care to hear his objections. However, he
prevailed and was somehow able to extend the
period of time given him for his stay in Germany.
The longer one remained in Germany, the less
one was permitted to take out of the country. In
the end my father and I arrived in New York each
with four dollars in our pockets in March of 1939.

Herr Guttman-Platau, a German-born Jew, had
more foresight or perhaps more insight into
happenings in Germany and, perhaps, he had read

Hitler's "Mein Kampf." He left Germany with his son and wife, my piano teacher, in about 1935. Before emigrating, Frau Guttman-Platau recommended that I continue my piano studies with Fräulein Epstein. That I did until the afternoon of Kristallnacht (Crystal Night).

Chapter 4

My father, a religious man, observed not only all the Jewish holidays but attended synagogue services with his children every Friday night and Saturday morning. Fridays my mother was busy preparing the Friday night dinner as well as the food for Saturday. She cooked fresh carp bought earlier that morning at the "Markthalle" (a farmer's market). I recall one occasion when she had to shop on Thursday. She brought home a live carp. We put the carp in our bathtub, which we had filled with cold water. My brother George, about three years old at the time, couldn't take his eyes off the fish swimming around in the tub. His curiosity prompted him to lean further and further into the tub, and you guessed it, he fell in. The cold water shocked him more than the encounter with the fish. He set up such a howl that we all came running into the "Badezimmer"(room with bathtub) and rescued him and the fish. Our cousin Felix helped in the rescue operation. Felix, the son of my mother's oldest brother Chamaier, was spending his summer vacation with us. He was studying textiles and design at a German university in order to prepare himself for running my uncle's textile factory in Lodz one day.

To get back to the dinner, my mother cooked the fresh carp with carrots and onions; she baked delicious challah (a type of braided bread); she prepared cookies and sponge cake or apple cake. The wonderful aroma of the baked goods permeated the whole apartment. The meal also included a chicken dish, potatoes and dumplings. An "oyrech," a poor man, usually accompanied us home after services at the" Storch," the beautiful orthodox synagogue to which we belonged. It was desecrated during the war, becoming a trading area where pigs and cows were kept and sold. Only recently did I come across an article in a Jewish publication showing a photo of the Storch in its full glory. Jewish philanthropists had rehabilitated the synagogue completely and had restored it to its former beauty and purpose.

The needy guest was seated with us at the Sabbath table. He delighted in the tasty food and regaled us with stories, showing his knowledge of the Torah, the Old Testament. The dietary laws were strictly observed which meant that the chickens or cows were slaughtered according to the way described in the chapter of the Mishna (code of laws) entitled "Bube Metzia." It dealt with laws concerning "shechita," the Hebrew word for the kosher way of butchering fowl or cows. The laws were very specific and were designed to spare the animal unnecessary pain. Generally, one had to be as humane as possible in the process of killing it. For instance, the person (schochet) performing this act had to test the knife used for sharpness and smoothness. He did this by running his thumbnail over the sharp edge of the knife. If he felt any imperfection, that knife could not be used. Now, among all the decrees that were constantly issued by the Germans, this one issued some time in 1938, or at least implemented in Breslau in 1938, went right to the heart of shechita, in that it strictly forbade the kosher method of killing animals. My father, an orthodox Jew, had never eaten anything that was not kosher. Taking his life into his hands, he would go to the farmer's market once a week, buy some live chickens, hide them under his overcoat and bring them back to our apartment house. There his tenant living on the second floor, Mister Pakula, a shochet and cantor would kill them according to the laws of the Torah.

Chapter 5

My mother, who had maintained her Polish citizenship, liked visiting her relatives in Poland during her vacations and would have one or all of us accompany her. The first time she took me with her I was about three years old. I got to know my father's parents then. They lived in a town called Skerniewice located near Warsaw. I remember my grandfather as distinctly as if I had taken a mental photograph of him. He wore a large round black yarmulke (skullcap) on his head and had a long gray-beard. He was dressed in black, and was always seated at the window, reading his siddur (prayer book). He paid little attention to me when I busied myself with one of our suitcases. I had dragged it to the doorway leading into the room thus blocking entry into the room. Now I was waiting to see what would happen when my grandmother came along. She, a diminutive figure in black, hailed from Rumania. Her maiden name was Adler, and she was rumored to have been a relative of Luther and Stella Adler, the actors. Entering the room, she promptly fell over the suitcase, which she had not noticed. I was very pleased with myself. Fortunately, she was not hurt, but I remember that scene as if it had happened yesterday, a scene forever frozen in time.

Photo of my father's family in Skierniewice taken at the grave of my grandmother. They all perished at the hands of the Nazis. The Nazis even destroyed the gravestone on which my grandmother's name was clearly displayed in Hebrew letters.

I recognize my Uncle Mailech standing in the top row on right; my Aunt Charne is standing in top row on left; next to her is her husband, a nephew of my father's and my uncle's.

The man on right with long beard is one of my father's older brothers named Schlamme. I also recognize my Aunt Sura, wife of Uncle Mailech. She is leaning on the gravestone on left. The young boy standing on right of gravestone below my uncle is, I believe, my cousin Hershel. He escaped by jumping out of the train transporting him to Auschwitz.

Three sisters at the grave of my maternal grandfather; from left they are: my mother, my aunt Charne, my aunt Hella; on the extreme left is the husband of my aunt Charne; my cousin Felix, the oldest of my uncle Chamaier's three children, is standing on extreme right.

The only survivors on this gravesite photo were my mother and the little boy standing in front of her, my brother Martin, as well as my cousin Felix. The two children on right also perished in the Holocaust.

This is the town where my father and the rest of his family were born. The peaceful scenery depicted here belies the atrocities perpetrated here by the Nazis against the Jews living in Skierniewice in 1940ies.

SKIERNIEWICE

A picture postcard sent to me by my cousin Professor Shemaryahu Talmon, when he traveled to Skierniewice, Poland about ten years ago, relates this sad fact: "Only broken pieces of stone scattered throughout what was once a Jewish cemetery, could be seen."

The same was true when he went to visit the grave of our maternal grandfather in Tomaszow. Only the photograph of the gravestones remain in my possession. See my cousin's writing on the next page.

I travelled into a past that is no more, going from Tomaszow Maz. to Skierniwce and now to Wroclaw/Breslau. I searched for the tombstones of our grandparents. But no trace. There are a few broken stones scattered in the two graveyards in Skierniwce, and the building (hull) of one synagogue is standing. A sort and tragic sight. Now I know better what Israel has been for me.

My maternal grandmother, a widow, lived with her daughter Feige in Tomascov, a town near the city of Lodz. They inhabited the building located on the family farm. Feige, my mother's twin sister, did not look like her at all. She was married to my uncle Selig, the only member of this family who had served in the Polish army. They had no children.

I met uncle Selig during a subsequent trip. My mother took all of us with her on that trip. We boarded the "Schnellzug" (an express train) late at night and arrived in Lodz about 7 o'clock the next morning. There my uncle Selig was waiting to pick us up. No border guards searched us as the train went right through from Germany to Poland. Only much later did I learn that my mother had had a considerable amount of cash with her, which was sent out of Poland to the Bank of England in Palestine with only her signature and no other information. When we finally received that money in New York, (it had taken quite a while to prove ownership, since only my mother's signature identified the deposit), it gave my father a leg up in his struggles to provide for his family in the new land.

We were all unaware of the danger we had all been in. Had we been caught taking money out of Germany (even though it was our own), we would all have been killed. My uncle put my mother and the children in a cab. He dispatched them to Tomascov, while he asked me to accompany him on some of his business errands.

He wanted to show me off, his niece from Germany, to his business associates who had flown in from London to discuss business matters with him. Not being accustomed to traveling all night, I was dead tired, and after being introduced to everyone, I asked my uncle if there was a sofa or bench where I could lie down and sleep for a while. I was shown into a room, which had a bench in it and I promptly fell asleep on the bench, sleeping until my uncle came to wake me. He had concluded his business and was now ready to take me to Tomascow. When we arrived there all I could think about was more sleep. A few days later my uncle again went to Lodz. When he returned, he pulled my mother aside and told her that one of his business associates was so taken with me that he was extending a formal proposal of marriage through my uncle. He apparently owned three apartment houses in London and was financially secure. My mother yelled at my uncle, "Are you crazy to even tell me this? The girl is only thirteen years old!" That concluded the matter except that my mother was somewhat curious and asked me what this fellow looked like. I answered that I really didn't know because there were three gentlemen to whom I was introduced, but I was so very tired that I could not remember any of them.

©

My mother's older sister Hella on left; the
other young woman on right may have
been a friend. Photo was taken when my
aunt Hella still resided in Poland before
she was married. Hella later perished at
Auschwitz.

Picture postcard sent to my mother by her twin sister Feige; see writing on next page.

Standing on left is my mother's twin sister Feige. Sitting at table in front of her is their friend Sallah Byrzonski. Sitting on right is my mother's youngest sister Charne. Standing next to her is her husband a nephew of my father's and my uncle's.

Translation
So you may
remember us
forever I send
our photos to
my sister
gutcia and
my brother
in law Isak
zelmanowicz

zum
Ewigenerinnerung
schikie ich
euch unsere
Bilder für

Meine Schwes-
ter gutcia
nehm mein
ch Isak Zelmanowicz

Tomaszow

den 29/11

Charne Ell   Gutcia Ell

My mother's youngest sister Charne Ell on
left. She perished in the Holocaust. My
mother Gutcia Ell on right before she was
married. She did not look like her twin
sister Feige, shown standing on left in
preceding photograph.

Photo of my uncle Selig taken when he served in the Polish army. He was the husband of my mother's twin sister Feige. He too perished in the Holocaust.

A fifth sister, Tante Rivke, her husband and two children left Poland in the middle thirties. Their last name was Spirytus. They were bound for Antwerp, Belgium, when they stopped off at our place in Breslau for a few days. My cousin Gutcia, who had the same first name as my mother, was my age. The boy was younger. His name may have been Sam. I don't know what became of them, as we lost track of them during the war.

Photo of my mother's sister Rivke Spirytus, her husband and children. Rivke is next to Hella in age. My cousin's name was Gutcia. The boy's name may have been Sam. They left Poland for Belgium.

Chapter 6

For a long time my father had had problems with his stomach. Once a year he would travel to Chechoslovakia, to either Gräfenberg or Karlsbad to drink the healing spring waters bubbling out of the ground. People came from all over the world to drink this water. It was there, in Karlsbad, (now called Karlovy Vary) that I met my first Americans. Except for the language they spoke, they did not seem very different from us. My father had taken me along since my mother wished to remain at home with the children and the maids and oversee the business.

With my father on vacation in Karlsbad

It appeared that the "Gerrer Rebbe," a Rebbe (rabbi) of great renown, was in Karlsbad with some of his followers at the same time we were on vacation there. My father had once been a disciple of his and told me that he wanted me to meet him. He also wished to consult the Rebbe, whose opinion he valued highly, about the situation in Germany. At the appointed time we walked over to the Rebbe's hotel and were ushered into a large room with a huge desk. Behind it sat an imposing looking man. He wore a fur hat, even though it was summertime, and what appeared to be a black silk coat enveloped his whole physique. After the usual greeting of "Sholom Alechem," (peace be with you), my father pointed to me and said, "This is my daughter Cilli!" As I had been taught, I extended my hand to shake hands with the Rebbe. He ignored this gesture of greeting and motioned to my father to sit down. I realized in a flash that very religious men do not shake hands with women.

Up to this point I had never thought of myself as a woman, but rather a young girl; I had just learned otherwise. My father had begun to engage the Rebbe in conversation about Germany. I decided to sit down quietly next to my father and listen carefully to what was being discussed. Apparently, my father had started to activate papers sent to him in 1933 by his oldest brother Yisroel. Yisroel had long since left Poland, the land of the pogroms, to make his fortune in America. In the affidavits, which were submitted to the American consul in Berlin, my uncle vouched for us. He swore that we would not become a burden to the state and that he would take care of us should we not be able to do so ourselves, once we came to America. We were given a future date at which to present ourselves to the consul in Berlin. Until that date my father could still change his mind about leaving Germany. And now, he asked the Rebbe what he thought! Should he leave everything and emigrate with his family or remain in Germany? The Rebbe's opinion was the same as that voiced by many others, "Hitler won't last. All the other Reichskanzlers (chancellors) who had preceded Hitler did not last, and who is going to take this madman seriously anyway?" So in his opinion, my father would fare better if he stayed the course and did not make a move. Fortunately, although my father considered this advice, in the end listened to his own counsel based on what was happening all around him in Breslau. He knew the time had come for us to leave.

What really gave him a jolt and the impetus to put Germany behind us was the departure of our long time accountant and friend, Mr. Bartsch, a German and therefore, ipso facto, considered an Aryan. One day he informed my father that he could not continue to work for us. His life and that of his wife would be in great danger if he did not refrain from associating with us. He also asked us not to greet him should we run into him in the street. This psychological blow affected my father almost more than the expropriation of his business, which by the beginning of 1938 was a fait accompli. Goering had made clear in the many speeches he had given that whatever Jews owned belonged to the "Reich" (government). This emphasis on "Reich" did not prevent him from lining his own pockets. Thus, in accordance with Goering's ideology, other property such as the apartment building as well as oil paintings and jewelry belonging to my mother and to me had to be given up to the government. The much larger apartment building across the street from where we lived, referred to as the "Freiburger 24" and jointly owned by my father and uncle, had already been sold for a pittance. It didn't really matter, for the money received could not be taken out of Germany. The "arianization" of our holdings was now almost complete.

I too was very much affected by Mister Bartsch's departure, remembering the many times I had hung around the large heavy desk where he worked on our books in the "Geschäftszimmer" (the room where business was transacted). It was the biggest room in the apartment. A rectangular bay window allowed a complete view up and down the Freiburgerstrasse. It was accessed from the vestibule through a door to the right of the table and chairs. Mister Bartsch used to tease me saying, "You know your father will give you this apartment house as a wedding present when you get married!" I always laughed at that. It turned out to be a joke for real!

By 1938 my school did not function anymore except for the lower grades. Only my piano lessons with Fräulein Epstein, my Jewish piano teacher, continued. A darling petite woman she was, always dressed in a light blue shirt and dark blue tie and skirt. Our two-track existence was no longer possible. We could not lead a seemingly normal, well-ordered life on the one hand while knowing the dangers, violence and cruelties which could be visited upon us at any minute of the day or night. New laws, decreed and implemented daily, were designed to humble and disenfranchise the Jews of Germany and eventually the Jews of all of Europe. Accordingly, upon our return home from our vacation in Karlsbad, we began to prepare in earnest for emigrating to the United States of America.

Chapter 7

Much paper work and many visits to Nazi officialdom were involved. I was chosen to represent the family because I spoke German like a native having, in fact, been born in Germany. My parents, on the other hand, born in Poland, had a very slight accent, something that would have placed them at a disadvantage in dealing with the Nazi bureaucrats.

We received permission to take my parents' bedroom set with us, as well as bedding and linen, our beds, and the dining room table from the Wohnzimmer. But we were denied the beautifully carved credenzas, leather-upholstered chairs and impressive dark wood table from the formal dining room. We were also given permission to take a number of plain chairs and one of my two pianos. The pianos had faced each other in the formal dining room where I had spent many hours practicing the piano concertos that I had studied with Fräulein Epstein. She would come to our place and play the orchestral part on the second piano during the weeks when I was recuperating from a near fatal appendectomy. My parents had waited too long to call Doctor Weigert, our pediatrician, when I complained of severe stomach pains. They attributed everything to an "upset stomach" after a big birthday party, held on my twelfth birthday. In reality I had suffered an attack of appendicitis resulting in a burst appendix. For three days I was on the critical list and specific prayers (Tehilim) were said for me. My brother Martin told me that my two aunts who had come from Poland for the celebration, cried a lot. God must have heard them and all the prayers that went up to Him on my behalf, for I started to recover.

My mother was allowed to take her Singer sewing machine along to America. She valued it greatly for she had been a milliner before she was married and had built up a business with a substantial clientele. Now she would sew hats only for me and for herself. When she was a young girl she had loved attending school. There she studied Polish, Russian and German among other subjects. Her favorite place for doing her homework was under the huge dining room table where nobody would disturb her. When her father died and left a family of five girls and four sons, who were not interested in running the farm, my mother could not continue with school. She was apprenticed to a milliner, so that she would learn a trade and would eventually be able to support herself. Her oldest brother, Chamaier, was in no position to look after his sisters and brothers for he was married and had to take care of three children of his own. He was busy running his textile factory in Lodz. His interest in textiles probably came to him from his great-great-grandfather, who was one of the Ell brothers sent to Poland from Liverpool, England, where the family had an extensive textile business. He was to establish a branch in Poland. My mother's first cousin, Leon

Ell, had researched the family history and discovered this fact. Like my mother, Leon grew up in Tomascow, but left as a young man to seek his fortune in America. He was very studious, became a lawyer, and subsequently a judge in Chicago. Years later I located Leon for my mother in Miami, Florida. He had moved there from Chicago with his wife Alice after he had retired.

On one of our trips to Poland I got to meet my mother's favorite teacher, who was truly excited to see her erstwhile student again and meet her young daughter. I believe I inherited my love of learning and studying from my mother. My brother Martin seems to remember that he was waiting with a relative outside the teacher's residence, while my mother and I were paying her teacher a visit.

Books and the bookcase given to me on my twelfth birthday (I had wanted the bookcase very much), as well as most of my music were okay to put into the van, built to specifications and sealed with steel bands. We were also permitted to include various items of clothing such as skirts, blouses and my mother's fur coat as well as a pony coat my father had bought for me.

A list of everything that was to go into the van had to be handed in to the proper authority. I was sent with that list and interrogated about it by two plainclothes men, probably Gestapo. They always were Gestapo when they didn't wear uniforms. Nothing that was less than three years old could be taken out of Germany. The two men were now questioning me about each single item and the length of time we had owned it. They prefaced their interrogation saying: "You know, of course, if you tell us a lie, you will never get out of Germany alive!" Except for my pony coat, I had no idea when my parents purchased what, but proceeded to give them the answers they wanted to hear.

I distinctly remember the day everything was placed in the van, which sat on a flattop truck, for shipment to the United States. Two inspectors had come to watch what was actually carried downstairs and put in the van. About the middle of the day one of them noticed a beautiful pair of skis (mine) leaning against the wall. He exclaimed, "What a fine pair of skis!" My father, hearing him, immediately said, "Would you like to have them?" The answer was "Yes."

I loved those skis. I had had to do a lot of persuading to get my mother to agree to buy them for me and let me go away with my class and English teacher to the "Riesengebirge" (a well-known mountain range in Silesia). My mother was always so afraid that some accident might happen to me too, as it had to our Bubi. We spent an unforgettable week in this mountain range in Silesia learning to ski and to keep house. We cooked, cleaned and wrote skits for our evening entertainment, for there was no television then. We also had to pay a visit to the owners of the house that we had rented for the week and provide an impromptu performance at the piano for their enjoyment. All those who could play well were called upon to contribute. Since we didn't have our music with us, we had to play by heart. I had decided to play the Rondo Capriccioso by Mendelsohn and was reviewing the music in my mind as we trudged through the fresh snow on our way to their place. Despite our cold fingers all went well.

Though I was not happy to lose my skis, they were apparently enough to make the inspector want to go down with his colleague for "a beer." My father had been waiting for this opportunity, which their brief absence provided, to secrete a few items in the van. He had been advised by friends to buy Leica cameras and try to somehow get them into the van for they would fetch a good price in America. So while the inspectors were drinking their beer, he quickly carried a leather suitcase containing five Leica cameras downstairs and personally placed them in the rear of the van. A number of other items made their way into the van while the inspectors were relaxing over a glass of beer. My brother Martin was sent to my father's friend, the proprietor of a nearby jewelry store, to fetch whatever diamonds his friend had on hand. Martin ran all the way and returned with three or four loose diamonds before the inspectors came back, and the van was closed and secured with steel bands. Now the van was ready to be shipped to Hamburg and thence to a warehouse in New York.

Chapter 8

We were vastly relieved when this was finally
accomplished and thought that all we had to do
from this point on was to wait to hear from the
consul in Berlin and travel there to receive our
visas. It almost didn't happen. On the night of
November 9th, 1938, pogroms of extraordinary
proportions occurred simultaneously in all of
Germany, later to become known as "Kristallnacht"
(Night of Broken Glass). Hitler claimed that it
was a spontaneous outpouring of rage by the
German people, a reaction to the assassination of
Ernst vom Rath, a minor official at the German
embassy in Paris. On the seventh of November,
vom Rath was shot and seriously wounded by a
seventeen year old, Polish Jewish student, Hershl
Grynszpan. Vom Rath died two days later. Hershl
had been very distraught over the fate of his
parents, Polish Jews, who had lived in Germany
since 1914 but had just been expelled from
Germany in November 1938.

Rumors of the assassination were whispered
about, but no one realized that Hitler would seize
this incident as his pretext to unleash a mob bent
on destruction. Synagogues and Torah scrolls
were burned. Jewish stores were looted and
windows smashed. Jews were beaten savagely and
killed. Many were interned in concentration
camps.

Neither my parents nor I had any inkling during the day of November ninth as to what would transpire during that night. And so I went to my piano teacher in the afternoon for my usual piano lesson. On the way home I met up with a girlfriend who walked with me. When we turned from the Graupenstrasse (Graupen Street) into my street, the Freiburgerstrasse, my girlfriend suddenly stopped and said, "Take a look across the street! So many people are in front of your house." I turned my head and saw a crowd of people standing around as if they were waiting for someone or something. I immediately replied, "I had better go see what is happening there!" With that I crossed the street and tried to make my way to the entrance of our house, when two uniformed storm troopers (S.A. dressed in brown shirts) addressed me and asked if I was Miss Zelmanowicz. I replied," Yes," whereupon they grabbed my arms and told me to come with them. I said, "I can't do that; my parents are upstairs waiting for me and would worry if I don't come up." They answered, "Your parents are no longer there; they were picked up an hour ago with the rest of the children." I was dumbstruck and started to walk along with them in total silence. When we reached our destination, the jail at the end of the Freiburger Strasse, a big Iron Gate opened, and I was led into a huge courtyard. Hundreds of women and children were milling about, some talking to each other. Suddenly, I caught sight of my mother, my brothers and my sister. I ran toward them and asked, "Mutti (Mom), what is going on here?" She said she didn't really know. At first, when five SS troopers (Hitler's elite in black uniforms) had banged very loudly on the front door and she opened it, she thought that they had come to take them away for something that concerned only our family. They ordered her to wake the children, who were asleep in the Kinderzimmer, located way in the back of the apartment next to my parents' bedroom. My brother Martin related to me that they had never been so terrified before or afterwards and that my mother was crying as she woke them and told them to get dressed. He also said that the SS men wanted to know where her older daughter was. She told them she didn't know, hoping that at least I would be left out of this nightmare. I now asked where my father was, and my mother explained that after they had been brought to the jail, which none of us had ever seen from the inside, the men were separated from the women and children and were being kept elsewhere. "What are they going to do with us?" I asked my mother. She shrugged her shoulders, but added she had heard some talk that we would all be sent to Poland in retaliation for the assassination of the German embassy official in Paris.

As we were standing there, mulling over our fate, I noticed that my mother looked very tired. She was now about seven months into her latest pregnancy and had been on her feet for hours. Only recently did I realize that there would be an addition to our family. No one had mentioned it and she carried very well. It was not a topic either of my parents cared to discuss, particularly not with their oldest daughter. As I was ruminating about these matters, my mother abruptly started forward, running toward a man while exclaiming "There is Mr. Friedländer!" I had met Mr. Friedländer on a number of occasions and knew that he was a German-born Jewish lawyer whom my father had engaged a few times when he required legal advice. I also knew that his sister had married a German, an SS man no less. He was also among the crowd in the jail. Apparently, Mr. Friedländer had rushed to the jail, bringing his brother-in-law with him, when he had heard what was happening that evening. He had hoped to be of some help. My mother dispensed with formalities and started pulling thousand mark bills out of her coat pockets and stuffing them into Mr. Friedländer's hands, saying, "You must get us out of here. Please give this to your brother-in-law and ask him to intervene!" She had had the presence of mind to take all these large bills with her, when earlier that evening the SS troopers had come for the family. Mr. Friedländer replied that he would see what he could do. He returned a few minutes later and said, "All right, come with me!" We followed him to the Iron Gate where two S.A. men stood guard. Mr. Friedländer told them to open the gate. They did and my mother proceeded to walk out with the children in tow. I was the last one in line and as I set one foot out the door, one of the storm troopers said, "Not you, you stay here." At that instance Mr. Friedländer put his hand on my back and literally shoved me out the door exclaiming, "She belongs with them!" For a second my fate had hung in the balance. I will always think of Mr. Friedländer as my guardian angel, sent by God to save me from a dreadful end, to save me from the monstrous happenings of "Kristallnacht," which marked the beginning of the most brutal destruction of six million European Jews by the Germans and their allies.

My father's nephew and also his brother in
law, for he married my mother's youngest
sister Czarne. His name was Avram-Yitzchak
Zelmanowitz. Both he and his wife and
children perished in the Holocaust.

Chapter 9

When we arrived home, my mother and I put the children to bed. With that done, we were wondering what was happening to my father. As we were deliberating about how we might help him, I had a thought. I said to my mother, "If what you heard in the jail is correct, they will have to take all the people they rounded up earlier to a railway station and transport them to one of the border cities. My guess is they will move them to the main railroad station (the Hauptbahnhof). Suppose we go there and take a look around. The children are asleep now. They won't miss us!" My mother agreed to come with me. It was a fifteen minute walk and going on midnight.

The inside of the main railroad station looked very much like the 30th Street Station in Philadelphia except that the stairways to the tracks led up rather than down. Entering the cavernous hall, we noticed a long line of people to the far right of us, near the stairway with the sign saying: "Track 3." Two S.A. troopers (brown shirts) stood watch over them with drawn guns. We both went closer and sure enough, my father was there in the line. My mother asked, "Where are they taking you?" My father indicated he didn't know but handed her some checks that were in his coat pocket. The one storm trooper noticing this started yelling at us, "If you don't go away this instant I will shoot you!" We turned around to leave. But I was not satisfied not knowing where they were headed and said to my mother, "Wait here a minute, while I go into the information office and talk to the official in there." I entered a dimly lit, glassed in room with a busy railroad employee poring over charts indicating times of various train arrivals and departures. Without even looking up he said: "Yes?" I replied with a question: "When is the train leaving on track 3 going to arrive in Beuten?" He knew immediately and answered: "At 4 o'clock in the morning." I thanked him and walked out to join my mother. It was purely a guess on my part to assume they would be moved to Beuten (now known as Bytom), a city right on the border between Germany and Poland. But that was exactly what happened as we later learned from my father. Since we couldn't do any more at the moment than getting this bit of information, we returned home, picking our way through all sorts of debris and broken glass. In the distance orange and white flames shot up illuminating the night sky. They appeared to be emanating from the reform synagogue.

Now the wait began. For five days we tried desperately to find out what had become of my father. On the fifth day, toward evening, while my mother and I were out, the phone rang. The boys were asleep, but my sister Regina, nicknamed "Puppe," had heard the phone and had come out of the "Kinderzimmer" to answer it. She was almost eight years old and understood the importance of what my father [it was indeed my father] asked her to do. He told her to listen carefully and get a pencil and paper so that she could write down a phone number that he was about to give her. He was calling from the city of Kattowitz (now Kattowice) in Poland, where he had made contact with a Jewish family

after escaping from the Polish jail in which he had
ended up. For three nights he and the rest of the
people who had been transported to Beuten in cattle
cars were chased by police dogs across the border.
The Poles did not want them and pushed them back
through swampy land. Unsuccessful in their first
attempt to push them across the border, the SS who
were in charge now returned the hapless Jews to their
jail cells in Beuten. They tried again a second night,
but again the Poles pushed them back. Finally, on
the third night, with dogs chasing the Jews as though
they were animals, the Poles had had enough and
interned everyone on their side of the border.

After a day or so, my father, who spoke Polish,
noticed a fruit vendor coming into the jail, carrying
a fruit basket on his back. Those internees who
had some change with them were able to buy fresh
fruit from him. My father approached the fruit
vendor, and speaking in Polish, persuaded him to
exchange his hat and jacket with that of my father
and permit my father to carry the fruit basket out
of the jail, pretending to be the fruit vendor. He
gave the man whatever money he still had with
him, saying, "You won't have any trouble leaving,
for they know you." And that was how my father
escaped from the Polish jail and made his way to
Kattowitz. He then found a Jewish family who
permitted him to make the phone call.

Puppe could not find a pencil, but saw one of my
mother's lipsticks lying on a dressing table. She used
that to write the phone number on the mirror at
the back of the table. My father said to her, "Puppe,
be sure and tell Cilli and your mother to call that
phone number as soon as they return home." My

mother was too excited to make the call when we came home and asked me to dial the number. I did and sure enough my father answered and told me that we had to try and get him back into Germany so that we could all keep the date we had been given to meet with the consul in Berlin. We were to receive our visas at that time, the first or second week in February. My mother now took the receiver out of my hand and asked my father how we should proceed to bring him back. He had it all figured out. She was to travel by train to Beuten and make contact with a smuggler (there were always smugglers in border towns) and engage him to guide my father back across the Polish border. She was also to hire a car and a driver and wait for my father at the appointed hour on the German side.

The next morning my mother rose early and said to me: "I want you to stay with the children and take care of them. I am going to Beuten but will return late tonight. I will not remain there overnight because if I register in a hotel and sign in, it might attract too much attention. The Gestapo would immediately question me about the purpose of my visit to this border city. If I cannot find someone today, I will try again tomorrow. In the meantime you are not to divulge to anyone where I am or where I went, not to the children, not even to my sister." She knew she could depend on me and took off. Late that night she walked in dead tired, without having accomplished what she had set out to do. For a number of days this grueling routine continued until she found a smuggler who was willing to undertake the risky task for a great deal of money.

She set up an appointment with the smuggler, returned home to advise my father where to meet up with this smuggler, then engaged a driver with a car and drove to Beuten with the driver.

At the appointed hour, the smuggler linked up with my father on the Polish side. He knew exactly when the border guard would pass the area with his dog. They started walking in the direction of Germany through marshland, when the smuggler noticed a tavern. He told my father that they had enough time for him to have a quick drink in the tavern before the next guard's passing. My father didn't like the idea but was in no position to argue with his smuggler who had, in fact, miscalculated the time element. As he exited the tavern, a guard could be heard approaching with his dog. They quickly threw themselves down into the mud to avoid having the dog pick up their scent. Luckily, they did not get caught but my father could well have done without that bit of excitement. When my father spotted my mother with the driver and car, he knew he was back in Germany and thanked God for bringing him back safely. The smuggler was paid, and my parents departed with their driver to return to Breslau. Worn out and dirty, they arrived in the wee hours of the morning.

We children were overjoyed to see our father back with us. After cleaning up and imbibing in some refreshments and drink as well as sleeping for a few hours, the driver said goodbye. My parents thanked him profusely. Besides giving him the agreed upon remuneration, they showered him with all sorts of gifts. My brothers and sister and I hugged him and kissed him for returning our father to us. We never learned his name nor did we ever see him again.

A new phase began in our drawn out exodus from Germany. My father had to remain in hiding inside our apartment. If he had gone out and was recognized and reported to the authorities, he would have, at least, ended up in a concentration camp. Officially he was now non-existent in Germany, having been "deported" during Kristallnacht to Poland, and the Germans kept very accurate records. We had to be particularly watchful that the tenant living on the ground floor in the apartment to the left of the main entrance door did not see him. That fellow had not paid rent for years, knowing that the Nazi party protected him for the spying he did on our comings and goings as well as for the reports he handed in on the other Jews living in the apartment house.

The remaining days of November and December passed without incident. On January the eighteenth we had to rush my mother to the hospital. There she gave birth to another son. We tried to decide what to name him. According to new laws passed at the beginning of 1939, being a Jew, he had to be given a biblical name so no one could possibly mistake him for a German. After considering many names appearing in the Bible, my parents settled on the name Don as in the two tribes of "Don and Naftali." I went to register his birth and name with the authorities and, if I remember correctly, they spelled his name "Dan."

We had at this point approximately three weeks left before presenting ourselves at the American Consulate in Berlin. It was sometime during those weeks that my cousin Sam came over to look at the baby and say good-bye to us. He had just been released from Buchenwald, a major concentration camp. Sam had been taken there after he was arrested during Kristallnacht while walking along a road near the city of Fulda. The road led to the farm where Sam was studying agriculture in preparation for his stated intent of emigrating to Israel. A storm trooper on a motorcycle passed Sam.

This is my cousin Sam Zelmanowitz, (later to be known as Shemaryahu Talmon). He may have been in his late teens when this photo was taken. He is now professor Emeritus at the Hebrew University in Jerusalem and is still working on the Qumran Scrolls.

For some reason unknown even to himself, Sam looked back. Becoming aware of his gaze, the Nazi turned around and detained Sam, questioning him intensely. It soon became obvious that Sam was a young Jew on "Hachshara," the Hebrew name for the program preparing young, able—bodied Jews for agricultural work in Israel. The storm trooper did not care that Sam was getting ready to leave Germany. He arrested Sam who ended up in Buchenwald. Sam never spoke about his forced detainment at Buchenwald. The only visible signs of what he had been through at the camp were a shaven head and a new sadness of expression emanating from his eyes, as he embraced all of us and left.

Chapter 10

The day of our trip to Berlin arrived. On about the tenth of February we all piled into a cab bringing us to the Hauptbahnhof where we boarded a train to Berlin. The next morning, as we approached the American Consulate with great anticipation, we noticed long lines of people trying to get in to see the consul. Since we had a previous appointment, we were told to come around to a side entrance whence we were ushered into the waiting room of the American Consulate. Our trials and tribulations were about to come to an end. My father announced us to the secretary but nothing happened for a considerable amount of time. When was the consul going to see us? Nobody had the answer to that. As we were sitting there, waiting patiently, someone came in and walked right up to the secretary's desk. He spoke English and I had learned enough of the language to understand what he was saying. It appeared that he was a visiting American congressman who was here to assess the situation vis-a-vis the Jews in Germany. I explained to my father that an American congressman was in the room with us and had apparently come to find out what was going on with the Jews in Germany. My father immediately ran over to the congressman to plead with him to intervene on our behalf with the American consul. I don't recall whether I translated or whether the congressman spoke Yiddish or

German. In any event the congressman understood the dire situation we were in. His worst fears had been confirmed. Apparently stories about the cruel and inhuman treatment of Jews by the Germans, which had leaked out to the rest of the world, were true. Without further ado the congressman went into the consul's office. Minutes later he returned with the consul who seemed unfriendly. In fact, he glared at us, pointing at the baby being carried by my sister and addressed my father, "You did not tell me your wife was pregnant; I will not give visas to all of you, but will issue visas for you and your daughter Cilli only. You will go to America and find employment. When you can prove that you are able to support your whole family, only then will I issue visas for them." We were shattered! None of us had imagined such a turn of events. It was truly a nightmare. We implored the consul to permit us to leave Germany together. He would not hear of it and the congressman, who had produced the consul for us, could do nothing more. And so, sick at heart, we returned to Breslau with only two visas.

My mother, who was quicker to accept the consul's dictum than my father, realized that it was the only avenue of hope for her eventual escape with the rest of the children from this hell that Germany had become. She asked me to accompany her to the office of North German Lloyd. This steamship company owned the "Europa," flagship of the German line, built in 1930 and winner of the coveted "Blue Riband" for being the fastest ship at that time. We purchased tickets there for my father and me for our voyage to America.

Luxury Liner S.S. Europa

Exhausted mentally and physically, my father was lying down and dozing, when my mother and I left. When we returned with tickets in hand, he said that he had dreamed the two of us would arrive in America on the twentieth of March. We looked at the first class tickets, the departure and arrival dates being indicated on them, and lo and behold, our departure date from Bremen was the fourteenth of March and arrival date in New York the twentieth of March. There had been no sense in buying anything less than first class tickets since money could not be taken out of Germany anyhow.

My father was known, (just to his family), as a dreamer of events that were either happening or about to happen. Unlike the dreamer in the Bible, Joseph with his multi-colored coat, he did not like to talk about his dreams. Only occasionally would he tell us something he dreamed or sensed. For instance, once he had broken out in a cold sweat and instantly had known that his father, who lived miles and miles away from where he was, had just died. Upon his return home, a telegram giving the exact time of his father's death was waiting for him confirming what he already knew. More recently, he had dreamed about his brother Lipman whom he had brought to Germany, but with whom he did not always have the best relations. They would have disputes about customers (were they my father's or Lipman's?) and things of that nature. When they could not arrive at a mutually satisfactory agreement, they would call for a "Din Torah" (a decision to be rendered by a Jewish court). This court was presided over by a very learned Hebrew scholar who was Hebrew tutor to my brothers as well as to our cousins. All of us knew Rebbe Davidowicz well since he came about twice a week to give Hebrew lessons to the boys. He always wore a black hat and sported a very long dark beard. Tutoring was an important source of income for him. It helped to support his large family consisting of a wife and seven children. The two brothers, Isak and Lipman, respected him greatly and always accepted his decisions. I can only guess what became of him and his family.

The week before our trip to Berlin, my father became very disturbed. In one of his dreams, he had seen his brother Lipman in a striped prison uniform with a big yellow star on his right sleeve, sweeping the street. He thought about it and then, one evening after dark, he asked me to accompany

him to my uncle's house. We rang the bell and my
cousin Regina (she had the same name as my
sister) answered the door and invited us in. My
uncle and aunt had already gone to bed but were
not yet asleep. We walked into their bedroom, and
my father told his brother, "I am going to the
American Consulate in Berlin next week. I want
you to come with me, for I fear for your life if you
remain in Germany. You have the same affidavits
that our brother Yisroel sent both of us some years
ago and, therefore, you are on a list with a number.
It ought to be possible for you to receive visas and
leave Germany." My uncle was not interested in
going to America. He explained that since his son
Sam (Shemaryahu) was now in Palestine, he would
wait to receive permission from the British
government to immigrate to Palestine. He also
hoped that his other son Isel, who was in England,
would eventually be able to join them in Palestine.
His fate was sealed at that moment. The British
had no intention of allowing more Jews to enter
their protectorate, Palestine, which they had
wrested from the Turks. Already there were too
many of them on Cyprus waiting to be moved to
Palestine. Shemaryahu told me some time later
that he was encouraged by his then girlfriend
Yonina, whom he later married, to come to Cyprus
and help with the many immigrants waiting there
to go to Palestine. He shepherded a number of
immigrants whom the British had permitted to
leave Cyprus and brought them to Palestine. Upon
his arrival there Golde Mair told him that rather
than fighting in an army unit he would do more

good if he returned to Cyprus. He was to organize classes on Cyprus so that the Jews waiting there to be brought to Palestine could spend their time constructively by studying the Hebrew language. It had changed from a dead language used only for prayer (not unlike Latin) to a spoken language. He also had the task of aiding as many Jews as possible to surreptitiously leave Cyprus and transport them to Palestine on whatever ships were available. He became the prototype for the character of Ari Ben Canaan in Leon Uris's novel "Exodus." When the novel was made into a movie, Paul Newman played the role of Ari. Unfortunately, Shemaryahu, who occupied an important position in the Haganah and who had helped many Jews, could do nothing for his parents and sisters in Germany.

My father, who had unsuccessfully tried to persuade his brother to come with us, at least to Berlin, (not realizing what a disaster that would have been), said goodbye to my mother and the children at home. He did not want them to accompany us to the Hauptbahnhof. With heavy heart the two of us set out on the thirteenth of March, (my father's birthday), each with one suitcase in hand, for travel to Bremen, the port city from whence the "Europa" was going to sail to New York.

After checking out of the hotel where we had stayed overnight, we headed directly to the designated embarkation area. There, we had to get in line in order to present our passports and tickets to an official in charge of handing out boarding passes. When our names were called, we were suddenly pulled aside for questioning. Apparently news of the departure of a "rich German Jew and his daughter" had preceded us to Bremen. My father was led away to one office, I to another. Again, two plainclothes men pulled out the "list" about which I had been interrogated many months earlier. They immediately focused on one item on the list, the pony coat my father had had made up for me. They wanted to know how many such coats were in the van, which had long since left Germany. I answered, "One," whereupon they insisted that three coats were shown on the list. I said, "That's impossible, for I know that only one pony coat was placed in the van." They were relentless in maintaining that three such coats were on the list. Finally, I said, "May I look at the list?" They handed me three sheets of paper and kept pointing at one fur coat on the first sheet, another on the second sheet and still another on the third sheet. I carefully examined the three sheets of paper and realized that what they had given me was a page and two copies of the same first page. Apparently, they were on a fishing expedition trying to shake my answers by using this rather clumsy ploy. I looked up and handed the three sheets back to them saying, "You have here one list and two copies of the same list." They started laughing out loud, thinking that was a pretty good trick they had played on me even though it did not work. I guess there was nothing else they could think of, so they let me go.

I quickly walked up the long gangplank and positioned myself at the ship's railing in order to be able to see my father who had not yet come aboard. I waited about five or ten minutes. My father was nowhere to be seen. All kinds of thoughts were racing through my mind! Where is he? What have they done with him? What if he does not get to the gangplank in time? The various workers were beginning to untie the ropes holding the gangplank in place. I was becoming frantic, when I spotted him running toward the gangplank. He was the very last passenger to board this fifty thousand-ton ship. Though he looked pale, we both were vastly relieved that he was finally with me on the Europa. The ship's engines could be heard turning as the Europa moved slowly out of the harbor.

S.S. EUROPA

Commissioned in the late 1920s by North
German Lloyd, a steamship company, it won
the coveted "Blue Riband" in 1930 for being
the fastest ship at that time. In 1945 when our
troops entered Bremen, the home Port of the
Europa, they boarded the Europa, which had
been used as a troop ship during the war, and
took it over. The American Government then
gave the ship to the French to compensate
them for the loss of their luxury liner
"Normandie" which had burned up in New
York harbor. The French rehabilitated the ship
and renamed the Europa "Liberté." Under that
name it continued to ply the oceans again as a
passenger ship until 1965, when it had become
outdated and was discarded as scrap. (See:
The Classic Liners of Long Ago-Europa)
http:www.schuminweb.com/ocean-liners/
europa.htm

This photo shows my cousin shemeryahu conducting a seminar in his house. The seminar was attended by Ben Gurion among others.

My cousin Shemaryahu Talmon giving a seminar at his home. The seminar was attended by Ben Gurion as well as by others.

Chapter 11

After locating our stateroom, we rested up from this last ordeal; then I asked my father what had taken him so long. He told me that the two men who had led him away searched him several times. When they could find nothing hidden on his person, they told him to dress. He put on his trousers, shirt, vest and jacket. At that point they started eyeing his gold pocket watch and chain. One of them said, "You are wearing a very nice gold watch. We sure would like such a watch." My father immediately took his watch out of his vest pocket and gave it to them. He knew that they would not have let him go otherwise.

We settled into a routine, taking the elevator to the proper floor where the meals were served and even having tea in the afternoon in an elegant café, watching couples whirl by as they danced to the sounds of the band. An American returning from a visit to Europe had made the acquaintance of my father earlier. He joined us at our table, and as the men were chatting, a German walked over to us and asked me to dance. I did not quite know how to handle this situation and quickly glanced at my father. He shook his head ever so slightly. I understood and said, "Nein danke; Ich kann ja nicht tanzen" (No thanks; I don't know how to dance.) What absurd irony, I thought! A German asking me to dance with him in this almost surrealistic setting of the café, pretending to be a gentleman, pretending to behave in a civil manner towards Jews (I am sure that he knew what we were).

My father read my thoughts and added, "I don't trust those criminals, for as long as we are on a German ship, we are not yet safe. They can always call the ship back. Only when I set foot on American soil will I feel free of them." My father instinctively knew what was learned some years later, that the Europa like her sister ship the Bremen, was a courier, carrying German spies to New York. An engineer on the Europa and steward Karl Schlueter became agents for the "Abwehr", the super secret espionage agency with headquarters in Hamburg and a branch in Bremen. A steward on the Bremen also offered his services to the super secret "Abwehr". Documents stolen from outfits like Sperry and Norden by workers who spied for their fatherland (although they had for some time been U.S. citizens,) were given mostly to Karl Schlueter, the steward in first class of the Europa. The spies usually met at the Taft hotel in Manhattan. The head of this particular spy ring was Dr. Griebl who maintained an office in Yorkville (a neighborhood in New York City with a large German population) and recruited many operatives there. Mr. Schlueter, when returning on the Europa to Bremen, delivered the stolen blueprints, drawings and many other documents to the Abwehr. Under its chief, Admiral Canaris, the spies of the Abwehr specialized mostly in clandestine coverage of the U.S. and Britain[1].

After the incident in the ship's café, we avoided going there and spent most of our time on deck,

---

[1] Farago,Ladislas, The Game of the Foxes, David McKay Company, New York,1971, Bantam edition, published February 1973, pp. 28-41

taking walks and watching the towering waves roll
up against the ship's walls and dissolve in an
endless repetitive pattern.

All we really thought about and talked about was
"Mutti." How was she managing without us there to
help? Were the boys and Puppe behaving or were
they giving her a hard time? Thinking about Meta,
(our last maid), gave us some comfort. Although
she had had to stop working for us, she had never
stopped visiting. When she got married, she brought
her new husband to meet us telling him how much
she had loved being part of our household. He was
a nice young man (not wearing any Nazi uniform)
and he was unemployed. At the time my father had
lost his old janitor, Mr. Schaebel, who had died. Being
in need of a replacement my father offered the
young couple the job of janitors for the building.
The position would provide them with a small
apartment on the ground floor in addition to a salary.
They accepted immediately at some risk to
themselves. The arrangement worked out well for
both of us. When we were about to leave, Meta came
up to assure us that she would help as much as
possible with the baby and take him for walks in his
carriage. She felt that nobody would bother her and
even if she were asked questions about the baby, she
would simply say that it was her baby. Since she was
married about a year or so that seemed reasonable.
However, she could not take the rest of the children
along. That could not have been explained so easily.

The fourth day out at sea, the Atlantic raged
with a terrifying fury. Waves racing toward the ship's
walls as if to devour them, merely crashed against the

ship, rocking it from side to side and hurling us against the cabin walls. The Europa withstood the onslaught. It was the only day I felt really seasick and could not leave the cabin, although the best remedy would have been to get out onto the deck. The fresh air would supposedly have made me feel better. The next day the sun pierced through the clouds and brightened the blue sky; all was calm again. I felt better, in fact, well enough to visit the dining room.

On the sixth day seagulls began to circle the ship, a sure sign that we were nearing land. Toward noon we were straining to see the Statue of Liberty beckoning in the distance. Excitement gripped everyone. For us it meant the day of deliverance was near. Two tugboats appeared. They were to guide this behemoth of a ship into New York harbor. It did not take long for the engines to grind to a halt. We had arrived!

Part II

AMERICA

"NEARLY DOWN FOR THE COUNT,
THEY ROSE TO NEW HEIGHTS."

This is the title of an article, written by Joseph
H. Gluck about my family in the 1950s. He is
or was a journalist for the Kings Courier,
1962 Utica Ave., BKLYN, NY.

Chapter 1

My father had been the last passenger to board the "Europa," but he was the first to disembark, hurrying down the gangplank to fall into his brother's arms. Twenty-five years separated them in age and time, my father being the youngest and my uncle the eldest of seven. They had no problem recognizing each other although my uncle's face was now framed by a small gray beard. My Aunt Channe, truly an angel of love, threw her arms around me as if she had known me all her life. My two cousins Abe and Charlie, who had never met either one of us, welcomed us equally warmly, picking up our two suitcases and leading us to their car.

On the way from the pier where the Europa had docked, to Bensonhurst, the section of Brooklyn my relatives called home, we were all babbling at the same time. I was trying out my English on my cousins, my father was speaking in German, Yiddish and Polish to his brother and sister-in-law. The exhilaration we all felt pushed into the background (for a few hours) that which had preoccupied us throughout the voyage—the fate of those we had left behind and how we were going to bring them to America, this most wonderful country in the world, bar none.

Two more cousins, Aaron and Joe, awaited us in the modest second floor apartment in which my aunt and uncle lived. We were shown to a fairly large room with two beds, a chest of drawers and a small desk. For a number of months it became our home. Their dog "Lobo" immediately attached himself to me and began sleeping under my bed.

After dinner, which my aunt had prepared, a lot of people started drifting in and out of the apartment. There were friends as well as more relatives. Rebecca, my aunt's daughter, came with her two young children. She lived only a few blocks away and, like all the others, wanted to meet the newcomers. She was a very lively woman with a hearty laugh and a great sense of humor. She quickly became one of my favorite people. One family by the name of Moskowitz hailed from the same town in Poland as my aunt and uncle. They visited, bringing their daughter Edna and son Murray who became my best friends in the early years after my arrival in the States. The evening turned into a big welcoming event. After a while I had to excuse myself for I was tired from all the talk and all the introductions even though everyone was very warm and most friendly!

The next morning after breakfast, (which I helped my aunt prepare, wanting to make myself useful immediately), my uncle asked my father and me to come with him to meet some friends of his. They had played a crucial role in securing the life-saving affidavits for us. Being quite well off they had helped underwrite my uncle's guarantees since he did not have enough capital to show that he would be able to provide for us if needed. These friends lived in an apartment over a delicatessen store that they owned. The name of

these generous people was Nemerovski. The older
daughter Sylvia was married but worked in the
delicatessen store to help out. She was a very
pretty and friendly woman of about twenty-eight
and immediately invited us upstairs where we met
the younger son and teenage daughter. We
thanked everyone, particularly Mr. Nemerovski
and his wife, for this most unselfish deed of
support that they had given my uncle. It had
enabled him to rescue us from certain death in
one of the many extermination camps in
Germany. As we were sitting around the dining
room table, answering questions about what was
happening in Germany and why my mother and
the rest of the children were not with us, my father
noticed an upright piano. He asked if anyone
there played the piano. Sylvia said that she had
studied the piano for a while but couldn't really
play anything properly anymore. With that my
father turned to me and said: "You play something
for these lovely people!" I got up and started to
play. I don't recall exactly what I played. It may
have been Chopin's A flat major Ballade. They
were so impressed that I was immediately asked if
I would teach their younger daughter to play the
piano. I answered yes and it was agreed that I was
to come to their place twice a week and be paid
one dollar for each lesson. Unfortunately, I cannot
remember the name of this young lady, my very
first student.

Teaching music in the English language was a
bit difficult at first, for I had to prepare myself with
dictionary in hand and translate all the musical terms.
For example, A flat major was "As Dur" in German,

G clef was "Violin Schluessel," C sharp was "Cis" and so on. I rose to the challenge and soon other students, who had heard about me by word of mouth, followed to take piano lessons with me.

Sylvia, however, was not only interested in my knowledge of music. She thought that I should also continue my schooling, which had been interrupted, before I could graduate from high school. She personally went with me to the nearest high school and introduced me to the principal. After determining how far I had gotten in my studies in Germany, he decided that all I needed in order to graduate were a few courses in American history, a course in government and a few courses in English dealing with American literature. None of these subjects had been taught at my previous school. Upon completion of the courses I would have to submit to New York State Regents examinations. I began immediately, the next morning, even though less than three months were left in the semester.

Meanwhile, my father tried to start a business dealing with dry goods. He learned to take the subway, which at first ran on tracks above 86th Street and then disappeared into a tunnel. It ultimately took him downtown to his station near Orchard Street. There he made contact with wholesalers in the linen business and in other assorted businesses along those lines. He could not imagine himself working for someone at a job. His mind was totally oriented toward business. We both knew that the American consul in Berlin would not be satisfied with the kinds of work we had begun to pursue (he starting a business, I giving piano lessons). We discussed the matter with my uncle, wondering how to proceed to extricate my mother and the other children from Germany. He suggested that we pay a visit to an old buddy of my father's, Teddy Blatt. Teddy and my father had grown up together in Skerniewice but followed different paths in their late teens. While my father escaped the dreadfully anti-semitic Polish military by going to Germany, Teddy went to America where he availed himself of the educational opportunities, studying at night while working during the day. He eventually graduated from law school and was now an important person in New York government. We agreed that this was an excellent suggestion. Anyhow, my father was anxious to meet with his old friend and knew that Teddy would help, if he could.

My uncle phoned Teddy, who had handled some of his business affairs, to inform him that his erstwhile friend Isak had recently arrived in America with his daughter and would like to see him. Teddy immediately invited us to come to his office, the sooner the better. The next day we went by train to meet with Teddy Blatt. We received a tremendously warm welcome. The years of separation had not dimmed their friendship. Teddy was truly happy to see his old friend again and to meet his daughter. When my father explained the difficulty we were in, Teddy told us not to worry, for he was going to help and was indeed able to do so. He said it would probably take a few months, perhaps even three or four months before my mother would be informed that a visa would be issued to her and the children. But she would definitely receive a visa. We were overjoyed to hear such encouraging news. We had had no idea how influential my father's friend had become.

In our next letter to my mother we related all the events of the previous day and were almost incredulous that all this was actually going to happen. My mother was thrilled to receive the good tidings and answered that she could hardly wait to leave Germany and join us in America. She had had a difficult time after we had left. My brother Martin, ten years old then, had been jumping from one desk to another in school to impress a girl. He missed and fell, ripping the skin on his knee. To avoid telling my mother about this little accident, he pulled his knee sock over the injury. (He was wearing the customary short pants and knee-high socks). It did not take long before the knee became infected, and he started running a high fever. Only then did he tell my mother what had happened. She looked at his knee and leg and saw red lines running up and down his leg. She immediately called our pediatrician, Dr. Weigert, who fortunately for us was still living in Breslau. He informed her that Martin had ended up with blood poisoning, a major calamity then, since penicillin had not yet been invented. I am not sure how he was treated, but my sister tells me that she had to apply compresses to Martin's leg for days. Most importantly, his leg had to be immobilized and kept in an upright position. This was accomplished by placing a splint under his leg and wrapping his leg in bandages. He was laid up for several months.

As Martin related to me just recently, my mother had made some changes in their sleeping arrangements after we left. She had all the beds moved into the formal dining room, which was now empty. It permitted all of them to be together in this immense, high-ceilinged room. She also rented out the "Geschäftszimmer" as well as the backrooms to two Jewish couples. Having more people around her in this large, now deserted and desolate looking apartment, gave her some sense of security at a time when life had quickly become more difficult for Jews. Signs announcing "Jews and dogs not permitted to enter" appeared on all store fronts, including grocery and fruit stores. Often my sister was sent with a basket to the back of a store whose owner knew us well, to surreptitiously buy items such as bread, cheese, milk and butter.

One afternoon, while they were all living in the one room, Martin, lying on the couch with his leg propped up found himself alone with baby Dan. The baby was asleep in his carriage at the other end of this large room. Presently he started crying. Martin, wanting to quiet him, slid off the couch and propelled himself on his back over to the carriage. He started rocking the carriage and singing to Dan. Before long the soothing rocking motion and the singing quieted the baby who fell asleep.

Meanwhile, back in New York, I met some people who felt that I should have an opportunity to practice the piano myself. With that in mind, I was taken to meet a family who owned a grand piano. They were very cordial. After hearing me play they told me to come as often as I was able to and practice the piano. They lived on 83rd Street and Bay Parkway, which was just a short walk from my uncle's apartment. Their oldest son Neil attended Music and Art High School and also played the piano quite well. His main passion, though, was composing music. We soon became very good friends and so enjoyed playing four hands. He introduced me to some of his classmates and took me all over New York to acquaint me with the city. One day he asked two of his friends, Victor and Arnold, to come with us to the 1939 World's Fair in Flushing. Everything was so new and exciting! We wandered in and out of the various pavilions and had our voices recorded in the GE building. All of us sounded so different on tape that we barely recognized our own voices.

Deciding to get something to eat, we stopped at a hotdog stand and each ordered a hotdog. The girl who waited on us told us that she liked to guess where her various customers hailed from. She asked if we would mind if she tried to guess where we all came from. We told her go ahead! She turned to Neil and Victor and said, "You two are from Brooklyn!" Then she looked at Arnold and told him he was from Manhattan. So far she was batting a thousand. Now she addressed me, and hesitating for an instant said, "You are from the Bronx!" Everyone started laughing, knowing, of course, that I had been in the country for only a few months. We left without enlightening her about my origin, but I was thrilled to have been thought of as an American from the Bronx.

That evening I wrote an extra long letter to my mother; there was so much to relate. I also wrote to my former piano teacher, Fräulein Epstein. She and

her sister and mother were preparing to leave for
Holland. When I informed her about my giving
piano lessons and attending high school, she was
concerned lest I not have time for my own studies at
the piano. She felt it was most important that I
continue practicing, for she firmly believed that I
should pursue the career of a concert pianist. I would
have loved becoming a concert pianist but at that
time there were other priorities. I had to earn as
much money as possible, so that my father's friend,
Teddy Blatt, would have something concrete to show
to his connections, who in turn would influence the
consul in Berlin to issue visas to my mother and the
children. The other goal, to which I fervently
aspired, was to improve my ability in the use of the
English language to the point where no one would
single me out as a "refugee." I wanted to become
just another American and leave the past behind
me. But first and foremost I had to help my father
bring the rest of the family to America as soon as
possible.

It became all the more urgent when Martin,
having recovered sufficiently by the beginning of July,
walked along the moat on the tree lined
"Promenade" to the Königsplatz(King's Square). He
intended to go swimming there in an outdoor
swimming pool but could not get to it. For ten
minutes or more a column of tanks rumbled
through the city. Hitler, standing atop one of the
tanks, dressed in his brown S.A. uniform with red
armband and swastika, had his right arm raised and
outstretched in the familiar Nazi greeting. When
Martin reported this encounter to my mother, the

mention of tanks threw her into a panic. Having lived through World War I, she knew that tanks were a foreboding of something dreadful, most likely another war. She asked the young accountant whom she had engaged to take over the work Mr. Bartsch had left unfinished to call the American consul in Berlin on her behalf.

Between the many phone calls from the accountant and the pressure being exerted on the consul from our end through the efforts of Teddy Blatt, the consul was finally moved to issue the necessary visas to my mother and the children. She was told to prepare for her voyage to America. Deliriously happy, she thanked the accountant for facilitating her negotiations with the consul and conveying this long awaited news to her. He had not yet learned the Nazi greeting "Heil Hitler" and, as my brother Martin related to me, was apparently dressed down by someone at the other end of the phone when he simply ended his phone call by saying "Auf Wiedersehen" (Good bye). Martin, standing near the accountant, noticed that he became red in the face and blurted out "Heil Hitler."

Chapter 2

As soon as she actually received the visas, my mother went to the office of North German Lloyd and purchased ("Schiffskarten") tickets for their impending crossing of the Atlantic on the Europa. Then she set about packing their clothes, including mundane items such as diapers for the baby who was now about six months old. She decided to leave the big heavy baby carriage behind and take just a stroller. She wanted to travel as light as possible. Still there were at least four or five suitcases to carry.

When we received her letter informing us that she would be arriving in America on or about the 30th of July, we too were overjoyed. Her letter confirmed the good news, which had already been conveyed to us by Teddy Blatt. We immediately began looking for an apartment that we could afford and found one on West 13th Street in Brooklyn. It had two bedrooms, a combined living dining room, a kitchen and one bathroom. It would provide the basic needs of shelter, but was clear evidence of our greatly reduced circumstances. We were wondering how my mother would view this apartment. The monthly rent of forty dollars was all we felt we could handle at that time. The warehouse, where our van had been stored, was notified and asked to deliver our belongings to the West 13th Street address. As familiar pieces of furniture were brought up, I was particularly happy to see my own piano again.

By the end of July, my mother and the four children left Breslau forever. They followed the same route my father and I had taken in March. Accompanied by the couple occupying the former "Geschäftszimmer," they drove to the "Hauptbahnhof" in two cabs. After taking leave of each other and being helped onto the train, they were off to Bremen where they spent the night at a hotel before boarding the Europa the next morning. Their departure from Bremen and their boarding the ship was relatively uneventful, compared with what my father and I had been put through at the very last minute before boarding the ship. In fact I was told by my brother Martin, other passengers tried to be helpful to this woman traveling alone with all those children. Once aboard, my mother spent most of her time with the baby while the others roamed about the ship. They met some Japanese who befriended them and took photos of the three and also posed with them. My sister informed me recently that after the Japanese had bombed Pearl Harbor, my mother tore those pictures up. She didn't want anyone to think that we had had anything to do with any Japanese. She felt one couldn't be too careful. Ironically enough, she was proven to be right when we had to register as "enemy aliens", after America declared war on Japan, following the sneak attack on Pearl Harbor on December 7th, 1941. (I marvel at how easy it is now in 2001, for foreigners, many of them true enemies of our country, to receive visas and enter the United States of America).

On the 27th of July, the Europa docked in New York harbor. It was one of the last times the Europa made the voyage to the United States, for Hitler marched into Poland with his troops and tanks at dawn on the morning of the first of September 1939. England declared war on Germany a few days later, and WWII had begun. My mother had fled with the children none too soon.

Earlier in July, before my mother arrived, my aunt and uncle took me to Peekskill, a city on the upper Hudson River, where they owned a summer cottage. Many New Yorkers escaped the oppressive July and August heat by spending a few weeks in the environs of Peekskill. Here I learned to drive my cousin Abe's model T Ford. It had a clutch but no brakes. To stop this car I had to take my foot off the gas pedal and let the car roll downhill until it came to a standstill. What a way to stop a car!

My cousin Joe told me about their neighbors, the Stetsons, who lived in a cottage a little bit further up the road. Joe thought I ought to meet them for they had a piano in their place and I might possibly be permitted to practice there.

With cousin Joe and Lobo in
Peekskill during July of 1939

Cousin Joe a few years later in the
army and stationed in Mississippi.

One evening, Joe and I went up to the
Stetsons. Lilly, my aunt's granddaughter who was
my age, came with us. (Lilly's mother Anna was
my cousin, and though Anna was a year older than
my father, she always addressed him as uncle).
After I was introduced to everyone, I was asked to
play the piano. The usual response followed—
applause and flattering comments about my
accomplished impromptu recital. One young
man, a relative named Sanford Galat who had
come from the Bronx to visit with his cousins, was

particularly impressed and asked me for a date. I was not sure that my father would approve (I was sixteen now), but my aunt and uncle did not see anything wrong with my going on a date, for Lobo was to accompany me anyhow. One date followed another and another and continued until I returned to the city to help my father with preparations for our family's arrival.

The day before the Europa docked in New York harbor, I went shopping for groceries. My list included orange juice, lettuce and soft white bread. My mother and my siblings were totally unfamiliar with these items of food, since no one ate soft white bread or lettuce in Germany, nor did they drink juice, though we had eaten plenty of fresh fruit.

About noon on the twenty-seventh of July, my cousin Aaron drove us to Manhattan where we were to pick up the family. My brother Martin tells me they could feel the hot humid air as the ship approached New York harbor. It was a tearful but joyous reunion. I hardly recognized the baby, for he had grown so. We looked at each other, incredulous that we were actually together again and had all escaped the Nazi scourge.

During the drive home, Martin, George and Regina looked out the car windows trying to absorb all the new sights and sounds as I had done four months earlier. Again we headed back to Bensonhurst, but this time to our own apartment on West 13th Street. We walked up to the second floor of this garden apartment house. Off to the right of the entrance corridor was the bedroom my sister and I were to occupy. Then followed the living-dining room, which became the center for everything. It also served as the bedroom for Martin and George. George would sleep on the sofa, Martin on a mat on the floor. Martin did not mind sleeping on the floor for it allowed him to listen quietly to a fine short-wave radio, placed temporarily on the floor right in back of him. The radio was one of the valuables we had secreted in the van. My parent's bedroom lay beyond the living room and was fairly large, with enough space for a crib. My father and I had purchased the crib the day before they had arrived. A small kitchen and bathroom completed the apartment.

I don't recall what I had prepared for my family's first meal in America except that my mother was wondering what kind of food I was serving when I placed a head of green lettuce cut into quarters on the table. I explained that Americans usually ate a salad of lettuce before the main course. She also questioned the soft white bread we had all been unaccustomed to eating in our earlier life. I pointed out to my mother that the white bread would be quite tasty once I bought a toaster and toasted it.

Chapter 3

Leaving Peekskill for Bensonhurst did not deter Sanford from trying to see me again. He boarded a train one day and came to visit me, unannounced, at our new place on West 13th Street. That day happened to be the holiest day in the Jewish calendar, Yom Kippur. My father was more than displeased with this visit. How could a Jew commit this unpardonable sin of traveling on Yom Kippur! Sanford and his family were totally assimilated and thus it meant nothing to him to travel on Yom Kippur. He now had three strikes against him as far as my family was concerned. Realizing that he had made a faux pas he began to write to me whenever he had tickets to Carnegie Hall, inviting me to meet him in the city so that we might attend whatever performance was given.

I met Sanford occasionally, as time would permit. Since my family had arrived I was even busier than before. My mother needed help with shopping and taking care of the baby. Although we were all eternally grateful to be together in America, it did not alter the harsh realities of our situation, that first year that we resided in Brooklyn. It was indeed a very difficult year, particularly for my parents, who had to adjust to new customs and a new language, as well as start over financially in a country, which was just beginning to emerge from a most severe depression.

My father opened his first dry goods store on
Cropsey Ave. We were all in the store with him
one evening when two fellows entered and
approached my father. They demanded
"protection money." At first we didn't understand
what we needed to be protected from. Soon we
learned that unless we paid we would be subject
to all kinds of criminal activities. Stories had been
told to us about an organization called the "Mafia."
Now we had come face to face with their
representatives. Apparently we had rented a store
in an area controlled by the Mafia. Without
hesitation my father left that store the very same
evening and looked for another, more suitable
location.

He soon found what he was searching for on
Kings Highway, not too far from Flatbush, a very
desirable neighborhood in Brooklyn. As business
improved my father needed someone to help in
the store, while he was delivering orders or
traveling downtown to replenish his stock from
wholesalers on Orchard Street in New York City.
He asked me to come in and help. After spending
one afternoon in the store, I knew that I absolutely
could not do that. I told my father that I would
give him whatever money I earned from teaching
my students to play the piano, but that I had to
continue my own studies. I was now preparing
for New York Regents examinations in English,
American history and government. If they went
well I would then take entrance examinations at
Brooklyn College. Everything worked out fine. I
passed all three examinations with marks in the
nineties and in the fall of 1940 I was admitted to

Brooklyn College, a highly respected institution
at that time. Girls needed an average of between
87 and 91 to be accepted at Brooklyn College, boys
would be admitted with a somewhat lower average
on the assumption that boys don't study as hard
as girls do while in high school. My brothers were
enrolled at the "Yeshiva Ohel Moshe" (a parochial
school), while my sister started at public school.

By the spring of 1941, my father finally received
the money my mother had sent from Poland to
the Bank of England in Palestine. We used some
of that money to move to larger quarters. The
rest of the money was put down as a deposit on a
five-story apartment house. It was located on
Eighty-First Street near Bay Parkway. Both my
parents deemed an investment in good real estate
an excellent way of supplementing our income.
Rents coming in from tenants would eventually
pay off the mortgage. What my parents did not
count on was the hostility exhibited by most of
the tenants toward their new landlord, a "refugee."
Shiny new brass mailboxes were broken and
broken into several times. Other acts of malicious
vandalism occurred constantly because of the
animosity the tenants felt toward their refugee
landlord.

Once a month I would accompany my father,
when he went to the apartment house to collect
rent. At times my brothers Martin and George
would go with him. Collecting rent was always a
difficult chore, for the tenants made the most
unbelievable demands every time that he went
there. One couple living in our apartment house
was very pleasant, though. Like us, they had fled

with their son Emil from Hitler's hell. My father introduced all three of them to me. Emil mentioned that he too was attending Brooklyn College and had noticed me in the German seminar room, which was located on the fourth floor of Boylan Hall. I frequently went there, or to Taylor Hall, the college library, to study. One day, while deep in thought working on a paper for an English class in the library, Emil came over with a fellow student who had wanted to meet me. He was a language major preparing for a career as a teacher of German or, possibly, as a translator of German. This acquaintance of Emil was also taking some Japanese courses at Columbia University. Apparently he too had noticed me in the seminar room and had asked Emil if he knew me. When Emil answered in the affirmative and added that I spoke German fluently, he was even more anxious to know me. Annoyed at being interrupted in my work (I had so very little time in those days) I was polite nevertheless. Irving Elkin was the name of Emil's friend. If anyone had told me that this was the guy I was going to marry one day, I would have thought that person was crazy.

But Irving had far reaching designs on me and now that he had been officially introduced he began to cultivate my company. He would always sit next to me in the classes we attended jointly and would walk me to the next class or accompany me to the bus stop. Little by little I got to know him. He talked a lot about his plans for the future. I, on the other hand, who had enrolled at Brooklyn College as a music major and had switched in midstream to 19th and 20th century literature, had no particular plans except to learn as much as possible and graduate with my bachelor's degree.

Chapter 4

The summer of 1943 I spent at Camp Sequoia as their music counselor. I was also able to have the camp owners hire my brother Martin as camp rabbi, even though he was just fifteen years old and only a few years past his Bar Mitzvah. I assured them that he would have no problem conducting Friday night services and indeed he did so beautifully. Since he had a good voice, I also included my brother in the production of Gilbert and Sullivan's "Trial by Jury" which my campers performed for their parents at the end of the camp season.

Martin and I at Camp Sequoia
Summer of 1943

Two people, the dramatics counselor and the person in charge of making the costumes, helped in the preparation of this delightful operetta. I spent every day in the social hall rehearsing either the female lead or the male lead, or the chorus for their parts in the operetta. The night of the performance I conducted as well as played the piano from below the stage. Our rendition of the operetta met with great success and the parents rewarded all of us with wild applause. It had really been a lot of fun.

When Martin and I returned home we continued with our daily lives, he attending the Yeshiva with our brother George, I taking courses at college in the morning and giving piano lessons in the afternoon. I studied mostly at night and on weekends. My father's business kept improving and really required someone other than himself in the store. My mother, accompanied by toddler Danny was the one who would come to the store and help.

My father's problems with the tenants continued. He finally decided to sell the apartment house. The money realized from the sale went for another building, one that had a fairly large store with a room in the back. A rear exit door lead into a little garden. There was also an apartment on the second floor. My father moved his business to the new location on Kings Highway and remained there until he retired. He rented the apartment above the store and thus had just one tenant to contend with.

At almost the same time I persuaded my father to purchase a one family home for us. The idea of the privacy it would afford all of us appealed to me tremendously. I felt particularly happy in the music

room. French doors connected the music room to
the living room. When the doors were closed I could
practice the piano without being disturbed by
anyone. I had begun to take piano lessons again
with a teacher who was recommended by my friend
Neil before he left for Oberlin College. He had
received a scholarship there for musical composition.
We began writing letters in the fall of 1940 and would
see each other whenever he came home on vacation.

Meanwhile, Irving Elkin was still attending
Brooklyn College and was always looking for me in
class or in the German seminar room. I had made
other interesting friends at Brooklyn College, but
did not really have much time to spare for social
engagements. In fact in my junior year I had a
long talk with my beloved Dean Gaede, telling him
that I was contemplating leaving college to devote
myself entirely to a musical career. He did not think
too much of this idea saying, "You must have a
degree in today's society to get ahead in anything.
And, besides, with your brains, you should definitely
have a degree! There are so many others who don't
have half your brain who get degrees. So, you see
you must really finish and get that piece of paper."
He convinced me to remain at college and work
toward my BA and, furthermore, later on, advised
me to continue on towards an MA at Bryn Mawr
College. I had received a scholarship at Bryn Mawr
and subsequently a fellowship, which, eventually led
to a Ph.D. When I made the decision to pursue an
academic career I had to give up taking piano
lessons. There just was not enough time for that

anymore. Before leaving for Bryn Mawr I gave all my music students to a friend of mine. My parents no longer needed me to help financially.

My brother Martin, having graduated from the eighth grade at the Yeshiva, was now attending Stuyvesant High School. He too had begun to study the piano with Fräulein Epstein. His music teacher at Stuyvesant, Mr. Stuffragen, recognized Martin's musical talent and decided that rather than continuing with the piano, he should play the double bass. After trying this instrument for a month, Martin told his teacher that he really did not like the double bass and would prefer to study the cello. Mr. Stuffragen, a very nice man whose instrument was the cello, permitted Martin to make the change. He even promised to give Martin free cello lessons, if he would buy a cello. Martin had saved some money, for both he and George had been working on weekends at a catering place. With this money he was able to buy a cello. Every day he carried the instrument to school on the subway. (Nowadays a chauffeur drives him to wherever he needs to go from his home in Long Island.) The lessons with Mr. Stuffragen went well and Martin became quite proficient at playing the cello. After he graduated from high school he attended Brooklyn College for a while. But Martin was really more interested in business and determined to become successful at it. He reached his potential in the building and real estate enterprises he created. His three children all attended college and graduated with degrees in business. They have given Martin six grandchildren and two more are on the way.

Martin at the piano

George had returned to playing the violin and
was studying that instrument with his music
teacher, Mr. Ehrlich, at New Utrecht High School.
George was very gifted musically. Eventually he
advanced to playing the Mendelsohn as well as
the Beethoven violin concertos. Whenever
possible I accompanied him on the piano. The
three of us would get together at times and play
trios. My father loved listening to us when we
played together, but ran out of the house when
each of us was practicing. He could not tolerate
that much "noise" going on at the same time. And

when my sister Regina wanted to bring home a harp, so she could practice that instrument at home, my father absolutely refused to give her permission to do so. She was now attending Music and Art High School. I had prepared her for admission to that school by giving her piano lessons as well as giving her instruction in theory and ear training. She is the only one in the family who pursued a musical career.

After achieving a master's degree in music, she became a music teacher at a public school in Long Island. In later life she devoted herself to her first love, singing and performing mostly for older citizens who adore her. The music she brings to them takes them back to earlier and happier days when they were young and carefree. Her two sons also attended college, the older one becoming an attorney, the younger one a computer expert and golf pro. She now resides in Florida with her husband, a retired dentist. They are both very involved with the upbringing of their two grandsons.

With my sister Regina; the photo was taken at her home in Long Island during the time that she was a teacher of music at a public school.

My brother George couldn't wait to enlist in the army. As soon as he turned seventeen he joined up and was sent to Camp Hood in Texas. (I believe he needed my parents' permission to enlist at that age).

My brother George while stationed
at Camp Hood in Texas.

He met a lovely girl while at Camp Hood. She and her family lived in nearby Fort Worth. When George was released from the army after serving for only one year because he had developed an ulcer, she flew to New York to get some type of commitment from him. He was not ready for a serious relationship and would remain a bachelor to age twenty-eight. At that time he too had become a great success in business, first in photography and later on in advertising. He unfortunately died at age sixty-four leaving behind two grown children and a widow.

The youngest, Danny did not exhibit any particular interest in learning to play the piano. He took up the oboe though when in high school and became accomplished enough to play in the school orchestra. After graduation from high school he went on to Johns Hopkins University. There he pursued a premed course and after many years of study, became a plastic surgeon under the auspices of the Navy. He served during the Vietnam War as a commander in the Navy.

My brother Danny while stationed at
Portsmouth, Virginia.

His three daughters attended college, the oldest receiving a Masters degree in business administration from Fordham University, the middle one a degree in law and the youngest a degree in physical education. Danny and his beautiful and accomplished wife Madelyn, too, are grandparents. Their middle daughter Debra and her husband Doctor Andy presented them with an adorable pair of twins. The oldest, Tamara and her husband Jeff are also expecting twins. The twins are due any day now.

Chapter 5

Soon after Japan attacked the United States at
Pearl Harbor on December 7, 1941, my male friends
either enlisted or were drafted. A colonel, who had
come to Columbia University to recruit young men
who had been studying Japanese, noticed Irving
Elkin. After an extensive interview the colonel
promised Irving that if he enlisted, the army would
send him to Ann Arbor, Michigan, where he would
continue his studies in the Japanese language. He
would spend approximately eighteen months at
Ann Arbor as a private, but would receive periodic
promotions. Upon graduation he would become
a commissioned officer in M.I.S. (Military
Intelligence Section of the army) and then be sent
overseas. Irving decided to enlist even though he
needed only about twelve credits to receive his BA
from Brooklyn College.

He began writing to me as soon as he was
inducted into the army. To his dismay he was
assigned to Ft. Leonard Wood, Missouri, an
Engineer Replacement Training Center. For ten
days he found himself ankle deep in red clay and
mud, digging ditches, felling trees, etc.—Then
one morning someone realized the error that had
been made in Irving's orders. He was yanked
out of this engineering unit immediately and
dispatched to Ann Arbor, Michigan, to join the

M.I.S. group for which he had originally been selected. It proved to be a very rigorous course of study and periodically men were weeded out by higher ups. Only ninety of the original group of one hundred and fifty remained and graduated.

When he received his commission, Irving was given a leave before being shipped to the pacific theatre of war. He returned to Brooklyn and came straight to Brooklyn College, looked up my program at the school office and walked into whatever class I was in at the time. I was quite surprised to see him, but even more so when at the end of class he asked me to have lunch with him at a luncheonette on Nostrand Ave., a familiar eating place to both teachers and students. I agreed, though it meant cutting a class. The biggest surprise came during lunch when he asked me to marry him. I was totally taken aback since I had never even been on a date with him. I gathered my wits about me and told him that I could not do that because I was intent on finishing college, where I would be a senior the following year. But, I told him that I would go out with him while he was home on leave. I invited him to my house, so that he could meet my family. They liked him immediately! He looked rather dashing in his brand new Lieutenant's uniform and charmed everyone. The following evening he took me out to a nightclub in Manhattan for dinner and dancing and that's where we left matters.

On my first date with Irving at a nightclub in
Manhattan

Thereafter, many, many letters arrived, written
from various islands in the Pacific as well as in the
Philippines. While on the island of Luzon, he
reiterated in one of his letters that he would like
to marry me. He added that he would be the one
waiting and would definitely want me, if I would
still be around when he returned home. In
another letter he gave me an exact accounting of
his finances. I had little interest in what monies
he had saved and wondered how he could be so
practical and prosaic. I was also struck by how
definite he appeared to be about returning home.
There seemed to be no other option in his mind.

Sanford was drafted, and he too began to write long letters describing his activities and travels in great detail. He told me that some day he would like to show me all the beautiful places he had visited. I was quite sure that I did not want to go anywhere with him and told him so, when one day, while on furlough, he too dropped in on me at Brooklyn College.

Neil had enlisted in the Navy, but was permitted to remain at Oberlin College until graduation, when he became an ensign. He was now stationed at Norfolk, Virginia, and wrote a lot about shake down cruises. He explained that it meant taking a new ship for a test run and checking out all the different parts to make sure the ship was seaworthy. Since a great many ships came off the assembly line at that time, Neil and his men were kept very busy with that duty. Eventually, he ended up in Manila just as Irving did; Neil on a ship, Irving on land at Manila's Santa Ana racetrack. A million men were being assembled in Manila for the attack on Japan.

Meanwhile, back home, a girlfriend of mine who studied voice, suggested one day, that we could contribute to the war effort and the moral of the troops, if we spent one evening a week at the local USO. We would entertain the soldiers and sailors, she singing and I accompanying her on the piano and playing some solo pieces. I agreed that this was a good idea and felt that I had to make time for this worthwhile undertaking.

It turned out to be not only a contribution to the war effort, but a lot of fun, for we met some of the young fellows who were far away from home

---

and happy to be entertained by the two of us. One newly minted ensign, an engineer, was so impressed with my playing that he invited me to accompany him to a performance of Shakespeare's "Tempest". I accepted for I was taking a Shakespeare course that semester and thought it would be exciting to see a live performance on a New York stage of one of the plays I was studying. I watched a truly exhilarating performance with rapt attention. During intermission we ran into one of my professors from Brooklyn College who remarked that a fellow in a navy uniform was a fitting escort for viewing the "Tempest". Sheldon asked me for a few more dates before returning to Norfolk to join his crew.

Many letters followed. They were fascinating, particularly, when after the Japanese surrender, censorship was relaxed, and Sheldon was permitted to be more informative about the operations of his ship, the U.S.S. Concord. He wrote that throughout the war the Concord had operated from bases in the Aleutians, for the most part from the islands of Adak and Attu. The water temperature never rose above 35 degrees and winds of 100 knots were quite usual. After the atom bombs were dropped on Japan and the war ended the Concord was joined by another huge task force. They all headed for Japan. About forty miles from the mainland they were met by a Japanese warship and the surrender terms were signed. Then they all steamed through mine infested straits behind the Japanese warship into the harbor of the Ominato Naval Base in northern Honshu, Japan. While at anchorage at that base a constant vigil was maintained by our navy people. None of them trusted the Japanese yet. The third day they were anchored at Ominato Naval Base, a Japanese garbage scow came alongside the Concord. Sheldon writes: "They were a terribly shabby looking bunch, fighting for things like cigar butts, pieces of cloth and of course old shoes." Sheldon flew over the main island of Japan and was amazed at the devastation below. All he could think of was how could they possibly have mustered that fleet which had attacked us so treacherously at Pearl Harbor! And how had they been able to fight us for so long in the Pacific!

After a week at Ominato the Concord headed for Pearl Harbor and thence returned to Norfolk Virginia. Sheldon had hoped to receive some leave time during which he intended to visit me either in Brooklyn or at Bryn Mawr. Instead, to his great disappointment, he was ordered, the very next day, to report for duty on the U.S.S. Midway. Except for her sister ship the Franklin D.Roosevelt, it was then by far the largest aircraft carrier in the world. Sheldon, at first, was unhappy on the Midway because he had preferred the closeness with the crew, which he had enjoyed on the smaller Concord. He was also unhappy because he had been prevented from paying me a long anticipated visit.

At this time I had just broken off a long-standing friendship with Neil and did not mind that Sheldon could not swing a leave. I was not ready emotionally for this visit and was also very busy moving and getting settled at Bryn Mawr College. On the advice of Dean Gaede I had decided to accept a scholarship at Bryn

Mawr College as opposed to scholarships that had been awarded to me simultaneously by N.Y.U., Brown University and Yale. I intended to pursue a combined program in philology and literature.

Chapter 6

Shortly after arriving at Bryn Mawr College I met my new professors and my fellow graduate student, Sally Smythe. She became a very dear friend. Yes, we were the only two attending the seminars given in the library by professors Dietz and Mezger, the latter being the head of the department. We really had to be well prepared for each session, for there was no way of avoiding any task, hoping that someone else would be called upon. Our seminar room was situated between the offices of the two professors. Sally and I soon became aware of the great animosity, which existed between those two men. We had to be very careful not to show any preference for the teaching of one or the other. One had the habit of asking if a certain topic we had discussed was clear. Sally used to give her answer to that query to me when we traversed the campus on the way back to our dormitory. It was always, "Clear as mud!"

Both of us studied around the clock, making time only for our meals, which were served in our dormitory with our housemother in attendance. Each evening after dinner the housemother served coffee in demitasses in an upstairs room referred to as the "showcase." Male visitors were not permitted into the

corridors adjoining the showcase where our
bedrooms were located.

Mealtime gave us an opportunity to meet
students in other fields. Quite a few hailed from
other countries as well. Italy, China, Canada,
France and Egypt were represented among the
student body. At lunch I frequently found myself
sitting across the table from two Egyptian girls.
They seemed very friendly and told me that they
both were related to some minister in Egypt.
Being interested in foreign languages (I was
studying Icelandic and Gothic at the time), I asked
them one day to teach me a few phrases in Arabic.
I picked up various expressions and noted the
similarities between some Arabic words and
Hebrew words. Some months later a few of my
other friends, the two Egyptian girls, and I, walked
into town late one evening to get a snack at the
local diner. The conversation turned to politics
and I said to Aida Gindi, one of the Egyptian girls,
"We are friends, why can't the rest of the Arabs
get along with the Jews?" I was shocked at the
answer coming across the table from Aida. In an
icy voice she declared, "You and I can never be
friends." I knew then (in 1946) what the real
feelings of Arabs were toward Jews and I certainly
know it now.

Celia with friends at Bryn Mawr College

Sally noticed that many of the letters, which were placed on a table near the entrance to our dormitory by the mailman, were addressed to me. They came from fellows in various branches of the service and from various parts of the world. One day she teased me about it by leaving a note taped to a mirror above my dresser. She had written on it, "Do you really want an MA or would you rather have an Mrs.?" I laughed, for at the moment I was really intent on getting that MA. I made time only for what was absolutely necessary and answering letters was not high up on my agenda. When asked to teach two classes at Harcum Junior College I accepted. Harcum was just a short walk from Bryn Mawr College and involved only three two hour sessions a week. The money I was paid came in handy, for although my scholarship covered my room and board as well as tuition, there were other incidental expenses that I had to defray myself. I also tutored Patricia Acheson twice a week. She needed help with scientific German. Those long involved one-sentence paragraphs, that are so prevalent in German literature as well as in their scientific writings, were difficult for her to deal with. I was able to fit her in easily for she came to my room at Radnor Hall only twice a week for a one-hour session. Both of us graduated in May, she with her BA, I with my MA. Her father in law, Dean Acheson, then Secretary of State, delivered the customary speech at graduation, in May of 1946.

At the beginning of May I received a letter from Professor Bradley, head of the Germanic studies division at N.Y.U., asking me if I would be receiving my masters from Bryn Mawr at the end of this month. He also wanted to know if I would be returning to New York. If so, he thought I ought to get in touch with him for he had an interesting proposal to present to me. He had been involved in awarding me the scholarship to N.Y.U., which I had turned down in favor of attending the program at Bryn Mawr College. Apparently, he remembered me.

My mother and my brother Martin attended my graduation from Bryn Mawr. They met many of my friends and, in particular, my friend Sally Smythe and her parents. The campus was bustling with happy excitement as friends and relatives congratulated us on a job well done. Cocktails and finger foods were served to all the guests. I said goodbye to my professors, not anticipating that I would be returning in a few years to complete work on my Ph.D.

My brother Martin with me at my graduation from Bryn Mawr.

Martin and my mother left for the train station and went back to Brooklyn. I followed a week later. It felt good to be home again together with my

whole family. For the first time in my life I was
enjoying total relaxation and leisure. I was not
thinking about anything or anybody. That state
of bliss did not last long for I found employment
with HIAS, an organization which helped newly
arriving immigrants from Europe. I had to
interview them in their language, be it German,
French or Yiddish and then dispatch them to other
persons or agencies that would continue where I
left off.

One day towards the end of June I received a
phone call at work from one of my former
professors at Brooklyn College. He wanted to
know if I would like to teach two classes at the
College during summer session. I would have to
start immediately. I accepted on the spot and
handed in my resignation that very day to my
superior at HIAS (a rather unpleasant woman).

I loved teaching. My classes were very large,
about forty-five students in each class. They were
all veterans having returned after the end of World
War II from Europe and Japan. We met five times
a week in the morning. My preparation for each
class took three hours and consisted mainly of
trying different ways of presenting the material to
be covered, so that my students would find it easy
to understand and learn. Participation of the
students in the class was excellent and many hands
went up in answer to questions I posed.

A committee made up of tenured professors
would dispatch one of them to audit a class given
by a new teacher. In my case, professor Lasser-
Schlitt listened in on one of my classes. At the

end of the session she asked me if I had ever taken any education classes. When I replied, "No", she said: "Well then you are just a natural born teacher." After she gave her report on me to Professor White, the head of the department, he called me into his office and told me that he wanted me to teach five classes in the fall. They would be scheduled for the afternoon. I felt that I could handle this number of classes since three of them would cover the same material. However two classes would require a great deal of preparation since they dealt with nineteenth century German literature.

Soon thereafter, I decided to get in touch with Professor Bradley at New York University. I wondered what had been on his mind when he had contacted me at BrynMawr. At our meeting in his office he said: "We can offer you two classes for which you would be paid. We would also want you to continue here at New York University with work leading to your Ph.D. You would not have to pay tuition for the classes that you would be taking." I told him that I could not possibly accept this offer for I had already obligated myself to teach five classes at Brooklyn College in the fall. His answer was, "Oh, you can do it! We will schedule the classes you would teach here for the morning. That would permit you to teach your classes at Brooklyn College in the afternoon. You would then return in the evening for the classes that you would take yourself." I felt that this program he outlined would turn out to be an unbelievable load and it was. But he had talked me into trying it.

Summer session at Brooklyn College ended during the middle of August, after I had given final examinations to my students. A great sense of relief overcame me as I walked to the Ave. J bus and returned home. Since there wasn't a soul in the house, the intense quiet was most conducive to playing the piano. I began to review the Mendelsohn piano concerto, which I had played at a recital, oh so long ago. Absorbed in my music, I was startled when the bell rang, but got up to see who was at the door. I could not believe my eyes. There was Irving Elkin. Somewhat flustered I said, "Do come in". I had not written or thought about him in months. In answer to my query, "When did you get back?" he replied, "A week ago". Then I continued, "Why didn't you call?" He said that he had told his mother, that he was not going to see me since I had not written to him for a long time. Yet here he was with only one thought on his mind. Would I marry him? I think fate intervened at that moment, for I answered "okay." And then I added, "Let's go tell my mother, she is at the store."

When we walked into the store my mother opened her eyes wide and exclaimed: "Irving you are back from the wars and how wonderful you look!" "Yes" he said," and what's more, "I am going to marry Ceil." My mother glanced at me and realized that it was true. Now she could no longer contain herself and gave Irving a great big hug and wished us the best of luck. She was truly overjoyed that I had finally made up my mind and chosen Irving. Both my parents felt that it was high time for a girl of twenty-three to get married!

The wedding day was set for Sunday, the 25th of December, for that was the first day that I would be free; classes went right up to Christmas. Our one-week vacation began on the Friday before Christmas and lasted till the day after New Years. My wedding turned out to be a high point for the whole family. My parents, my uncle and aunt, all their children, my brothers and sister as well as Mr. and Mrs. Nemrowski attended. Also present were Irving's parents, his grandmother, uncles, aunts and cousins. And then, there were all our friends and my parents' friends, two of them from Breslau.

Despite the broad based indifference of the world toward the plight of European Jews, we, with the help of God, my uncle and friends escaped Hitler's "final solution". And like the Phoenix, we rose from Hitler's ashes, the ashes of Kristallnacht.

©

Epilogue

Irving and I were happily married for fifty-two years, when God took him from me. We led a turbulent and exciting life, traveling a great deal and living in Japan for a few years. While in Japan Irving took part in investigations that his CIC outfit conducted on various individuals suspected of war crimes. I became a "local civilian hire" and worked as a research analyst for the G-2 department of the army. In that capacity I wrote an in depth area study of a geographical area of great interest to us. When Irving's tour of duty was up we returned home to eventually go into business. Our two sons, Rick and Rodney were and still are a great source of joy. Both attended the University of Pennsylvania and graduated, Rick with a BA in Mathematics, Rodney with a premed degree. Rick continued his education at Harvard, graduating with an MBA, while Rodney attended the Medical School of the University of Pennsylvania and became a physician. They are successful in their respective fields and live fairly close to me. It allows me to visit with my five grandchildren (one a girl), often. The holidays are spent together at either Rick's home or at Rodney's. The five cousins love the family get-togethers and love each other a great deal. They all knew their grandfather Irving and shared the sadness we all felt when he passed away.

Bride and Groom on wedding day.

My wedding

My parents next to me, my aunt and uncle next to my father and Mr. and Mrs. Nemrowski at end. Next to my husband his parents and grandmother; uncle Ralph and an aunt of my husband's.

Irving's uncle Arthur standing in back of me and Irving; my mother and father sitting next to me; Irving's mother Rose next to Irving; another aunt standing between Rose and Harry (Irving's father). Irving's grandmother next to Harry; last in line uncle Ralph.

My uncle and aunt at my wedding.

The Couple celebrating their second anniversary at the GHQ Club (General Headquarters) in Tokyo.

9 781413 469189

BELARUS

Also by David R. Marples and published by Macmillan

CHERNOBYL AND NUCLEAR POWER IN THE USSR
THE SOCIAL IMPACT OF THE CHERNOBYL DISASTER
STALINISM IN UKRAINE IN THE 1940s
UKRAINE UNDER PERESTROIKA: Ecology, Economics and the
Workers' Revolt